ROBERT E. LEE

LEADERSHIP ■ STRATEGY ■ CONFLICT

RON FIELD ■ ILLUSTRATED BY ADAM HOOK

First published in 2010 by Osprey Publishing
Midland House, West Way, Botley, Oxford OX2 0PH, UK
44-02 23rd St, Suite 219, Long Island City, NY 11101, USA

E-mail: info@ospreypublishing.com

ISBN: 978 1 84908 145 0
E-book ISBN: 978 1 84908 146 7

Cartography: Map Studio, Romsey, UK
Editorial by Ilios Publishing Ltd, Oxford, UK (www.iliospublishing.com)
Page layout by Myriam Bell Design, France
Index by Mike Parkin
Typeset in Stone Serif and Officina Sans
Maps by Mapping Specialists Ltd
Originated by PDQ Media, Bungay, UK
Printed in China through Worldprint Ltd

10 11 12 13 14   10 9 8 7 6 5 4 3 2 1

Acknowledgements

The author wishes to thank the following for their generous assistance:
Patrick A. Schroeder, Historian, Appomattox Court House National
Historical Park; Jamison Davis, Visual Resources Manager, Virginia
Historical Society; Ann Drury Wellford, Photo Services Manager,
The Museum of the Confederacy, Richmond, Virginia; Meredith
McLemore, Archivist, Alabama Department of Archives and History;
and Peter Harrington, Curator, Anne S. K. Brown Military Collection,
Brown University, Rhode Island.

Artist's note

Readers may care to note that the original paintings from which the
color plates in this book were prepared are available for private sale.
All reproduction copyright whatsoever is retained by the Publishers.
All enquiries should be addressed to:

Scorpio Gallery, PO Box 475, Hailsham, East Sussex, BN27 2SL, UK

The Publishers regret that they can enter into no correspondence
upon this matter.

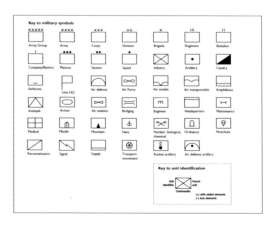

CONTENTS

INTRODUCTION

According to Winston Churchill, Robert E. Lee was "one of the noblest Americans who ever lived." He inspired an exhausted and outnumbered army to achieve greatness on the battlefield. He was a brilliant strategist and a man of unyielding courage who, in the face of insurmountable odds, nearly changed forever the course of American history. In April 1861, President Abraham Lincoln invited Lee to take command of the entire Federal Army, but the Virginian declined because his home state was seceding from the Union. Lee's initial role in the newly established Confederate States of America was as senior military adviser to President Jefferson Davis, and his first field responsibility was in northwestern Virginia where he took command of the disastrous Cheat Mountain campaign in July 1861. Unable to deal with the truculent General William Wing Loring, Lee missed an opportunity to score his first campaign success of the Civil War. He was next ordered south to supervise the construction of batteries along the Confederate coastline. The wise placement of these military installations prevented the North from penetrating many of the rivers and estuaries along the Atlantic coastline, and thereby prolonged the conflict. After the wounding of General Joseph E. Johnston at Seven Pines in June 1862, Lee was given charge of all Confederate forces in Virginia, which were renamed the "Army of Northern Virginia" (ANV). His greatest victories in command of this army were the Seven Days' Battles, Second Manassas, and Fredericksburg in 1862, and Chancellorsville in 1863. Following victory at Fredericksburg, he was celebrated throughout the Confederacy. According to the *Daily Telegraph* of Macon, Georgia, "No military man ever won, in so short a period of important service, a stronger hold upon the admiration and confidence of the army and the people."

Although Lee's victories against superior forces won him enduring fame as a skillful and daring battlefield tactician, there were inevitable weaknesses in the man and his strategy.

Two attempts to invade the North ended unsuccessfully. Barely escaping defeat at Antietam in 1862, he was forced to withdraw south. In July 1863 he was again worsted, at Gettysburg in Pennsylvania. His insistence on a full frontal assault on the Federal center on Cemetery Ridge on the third day of that battle was his greatest failure, although it might have succeeded if the attack of General Richard S. Ewell on the Federal right flank had been successful. It was only due to ineffectual pursuit by General George Meade, commander of Federal forces, that he managed to once again extricate the ANV and escape south.

Lee was also guilty of being too preoccupied with the war in the east while his key adversary during the last year of the war understood the importance of capturing the Mississippi River. In the spring of 1864, General Ulysses S. Grant, the new Federal commander, came east to begin a series of campaigns which

finally wore down Lee's army in order to at last capture the Confederate capital. In the overland campaign of 1864 and the siege of Petersburg in 1864–65, Lee's determination resulted in the infliction of heavy casualties on Grant's larger army, but he was unable to replace his own losses or prevent an inevitable Confederate collapse.

Various bouts of illness and injury, including a heart attack in April 1863, contributed much to the decline in Lee's ability to command towards the end of the Civil War. Lee himself was well aware of his frailties. During the invasion of Maryland in September 1862, a fellow officer informed him how trusted he was by the Confederacy and that he had "the hearts of his soldiers, and possessed the entire confidence of his country, and that the Army, the Government, and the People relied implicitly upon his patriotism and genius." In response, tears rushed to Lee's eyes and he exclaimed: "Do not say that. I am sensible of my weakness, and such a responsibility as your remark implies would crush me to the earth." Despite his foibles, the quality of Robert E. Lee as an outstanding general and tactician remains as a lasting monument to his success. At the height of his military career following his victory at Second Manassas in 1862, he was rightfully lauded throughout the Confederacy as "General Lee the Rising Man" and compared to "the Hannibals, the Caesars, the Fredericks and the Napoleons of history."

Joseph E. Johnston was initially assigned to command at Harpers Ferry, and shortly after combined forces with P. G. T. Beauregard to gain the Confederate victory at First Manassas on July 21, 1861. His wounding at Seven Pines on June 1, 1862 gave Lee the opportunity to prove his real worth as a field commander. (US National Archives 111-B-1782)

FORMATIVE YEARS

Born into Virginia aristocracy on January 19, 1807 at Stratford Hall Plantation, Westmoreland County, Virginia, Robert Edward Lee was the fifth child of Henry "Light-Horse Harry" Lee and his second wife, Ann Hill Lee, née Carter. His mother grew up at the Shirley Plantation, an elegant home in Virginia, and her father, Robert "King" Carter, was the wealthiest man in the colonies.

Young Robert did not have a happy childhood. Losing his fortune and home to bankruptcy caused by irresponsible land speculation, his father landed in debtor's prison. Further imprisonment followed his support of a Baltimore critic of the impending War of 1812 with England. Following this he sought refuge in the West Indies to overcome injuries sustained from a severe beating received from irate citizens, and died of his injuries on return to the US in 1818 on the Georgia plantation of his former Revolutionary commander, Nathaniel Greene.

Meanwhile, Robert's mother developed tuberculosis and narcolepsy, and became a confirmed invalid. With his older brothers and sisters and half-brothers and sisters either involved in their own careers or ill themselves, many of the "domestic cares" fell on Robert. Hence, he was described by Armistead L. Long, his Civil War secretary, as "old beyond his years, and of a thoughtfulness, a sense of filial obligation, and a warm affection for his parents that aided him to accept responsibilities and perform duties of which few boys of his age would have been capable." Lee would also spend later years nursing an ailing wife. According to biographer Douglas Freeman, "The man who was to order Pickett's charge at Gettysburg got part of his preparation for war by nursing sick women."

Lee was only 11 years old when his father died, leaving the family in debt. When he was three years old, his older half-brother Henry "Black-Horse" Lee, the heir to the Stratford Hall Plantation, having reached his majority, established Stratford as his home. Meanwhile, the rest of the family moved to Alexandria, Virginia, where the young Robert grew up in the houses of various relatives. A devout Christian, his mother oversaw his religious instruction at Christ Episcopal Church in Alexandria. Receiving a classical education at the Alexandria Academy, he was considered a first-class student. One of his cousins recalled:

I remember him well as a boy at school to Mr. [William B.] Leary at the Alexandria Academy, and afterward at school to Mr. [Benjamin] Hallowell when his school was in the house now occupied by Mr. Turner, and his mother lived next door. I recollect his uniformly correct deportment at school and elsewhere, and his attention to his studies.

Robert E. Lee's father, Henry "Light-Horse Harry" Lee was still a hero of the American Revolution, a friend of George Washington, and a governor and congressman when this portrait was painted by Charles Willson Peale (1741–1827) in 1782. (Courtesy of Independence National Historical Park Collection, National Park Service, Philadelphia)

What impressed me most in my youthful days was his devotion to his mother, who, as you know, was for many years an invalid; she used to say he was son and daughter to her. He was her housekeeper, relieved her of all domestic cares, looked after the horses, rode out in the carriage with her, and did the marketing for the family.

Lee studied the rudiments of a classical education for about three years under Leary, for whom he developed an enduring respect. He became so well grounded in Latin via the reading of Tacitus and Cicero that he never quite forgot the language, though he did not study it after he was 17 years of age. He also shone in mathematics and, according to Freeman, his "mind was already of the type that delighted in the precise reasoning of algebra and geometry."

Having reached an age when he had to decide upon a career or vocation, and possessing a natural tendency toward military science, Robert chose the military profession and decided to prepare for admission to the United States Military Academy at West Point, New York. His main instructor during this course of study, Benjamin Hallowell, described him as "a most exemplary student in every respect. He was never behind-time at his studies; never failed in a single recitation; was perfectly observant of the rules and regulations of the institution; was gentlemanly, unobtrusive, and respectful in all his deportment to teachers and his fellow-students… The same traits he exhibited at my school he carried with him to West Point, where, I have been told, he never received a mark of demerit, and graduated at the head of his class."

Robert E. Lee, aged 38, with his eight-year-old son William Henry Fitzhugh "Rooney" Lee. A cavalry officer during the Civil War, "Rooney" would command a cavalry division during the last days of the Confederacy. (Virginia Historical Society)

EARLY MILITARY LIFE, 1825–61

In 1825, when he was 18 years of age, Robert E. Lee entered West Point as a cadet. Little is known regarding his life while at that institution. He was undoubtedly an earnest and diligent student who was too absorbed in his studies to indulge in many social activities. With regard to his academic progress, he became the first cadet to achieve the rank of sergeant at the end of his first year. When he graduated in 1829 he was first in his class in artillery and tactics, and shared the distinction with five other cadets of having received no demerits during the four-year course of instruction. Overall, he ranked second in his class of 46.

He was commissioned as a brevet second lieutenant in the Corps of Engineers on July 1, 1829, and served for about 17 months supervising the construction of much of Fort Pulaski on Cockspur Island, Georgia, where Major Samuel Babcock, his superior officer, found him to be "in a measure inexperienced" but "active and intelligent." In 1831, he was transferred to Fortress Monroe at the tip of the Virginia Peninsula and played a major role in the final construction of that post and Fort Calhoun, later renamed Fort Wool, which was built on a man-made island in the navigational channel from Old Point Comfort in the middle of the mouth of Hampton Roads. When construction was completed in 1834, Fortress Monroe was referred to as the "Gibraltar of Chesapeake Bay," and would serve as a major base of operations against the Confederacy during the Civil War.

While he was stationed at Fortress Monroe, Lee married Mary Anna Randolph Custis (1808–73), great-granddaughter of Martha Washington by her first husband Daniel Parke Custis, and step-great-granddaughter of George Washington, the first president of the United States. They were married on June 30, 1831 at Arlington House, the home of her parents, which was situated just across the Potomac River from Washington, DC. While resident at Fortress Monroe, the Lees produced their first child, George Washington Custis Lee, nick-named "Boo," who would serve as a major-general in the Confederate Army during the Civil War, and also as an aide-de-camp to President Jefferson Davis. Their other children were Mary Custis Lee, William Henry Fitzhugh "Rooney" Lee, Anne Carter Lee, Eleanor Agnes Lee, Robert E. Lee, Jr., and Mildred Childe Lee.

Appointed an assistant in the chief engineer's office in Washington, DC, from 1834 to 1837, Robert E. Lee spent the summer of 1835 helping to establish the line of demarcation between the state of Ohio and Michigan territory. He received a commission as a first lieutenant on September 21, 1836, and next supervised the engineering work for St Louis' harbor and for the upper Mississippi and Missouri rivers. An important assignment during this period was the blasting of a channel through the Des Moines Rapids on the Mississippi by Keokuk, Iowa, where the mean depth of 2.4ft (73cm) had been the upper limit of steamboat traffic on the river. Although Congress failed to provide sufficient funds for the completion of this project, the respect Lee earned while undertaking this work earned him a promotion to captain on July 7, 1838.

In 1842, Captain Robert E. Lee was ordered to New York City where he planned and supervised repairs and changes to Fort Lafayette and the battery on the Narrows (later known as Fort Hamilton), between the upper and the lower bays of New York harbor. In 1845 he received an appointment as a member of the board of engineers for the Atlantic coast defenses. Without being relieved of his assignment at the Narrows, Lee joined with brother officers of the board – which included Colonel Sylvanus Thayer, his old superintendent at West Point – in studying the best method of fortifying Sandy Hook, in examining the entire defensive system of New York, and in forming a project for occupying the site of old Forts Tompkins and Richmond.

Lee was intent on another year of the formalized routine of an army engineer when war broke out between the US and Mexico on May 13, 1846.

On August 19, he received orders from the Chief of Engineers, Joseph G. Totten, to hand over his work in New York to Major Richard Delafield, proceed via Washington, DC, to San Antonio de Bexar, Texas, and report to Brigadier-General John E. Wool for service in Mexico. Transferred to the command of General Winfield Scott on January 16, 1847, Lee took part in the siege and capture of Vera Cruz and the 240-mile (386km) advance to Mexico City. During preparations for the siege of Vera Cruz, he was almost killed by friendly fire as he returned to camp with future Confederate comrade Lieutenant P. G. T. Beauregard through a narrow path cut through brush after supervising the construction of a battery. At a turn in the path, they suddenly saw the figure of a US sentinel, who opened fire thinking the Mexicans were upon him. Passing between Lee's left arm and his body, the ball singed his uniform. According to biographer Freeman, "A deviation of a fraction of an inch in the soldier's aim would have changed some very important chapters in the history of the United States."

On the morning of March 24, 1847, Lee aimed a weapon at a foe for the first time in more than 22 years of military service when the masked naval battery he was supervising responded to fire directed at it by the Mexican artillery in the defense works of Vera Cruz. Following the capitulation of Vera Cruz on March 27, Lee got his first mention in dispatches when General Scott included him among those who were "isolated by rank or position as well as by noble services." In a later report following further US success at Cerro Gordo, Scott wrote of Lee: "This officer, greatly distinguished [himself]

Engravings of Robert E. Lee and Thomas J. Jackson published in the *Illustrated London News* on February 14, 1863. (Author's collection)

at the siege of Vera Cruz." Upon the departure of Totten, Lee became second ranking engineer officer on Scott's staff, and during subsequent operations seems to have been consulted by the commanding general much more than was Major John L. Smith, the senior engineer, who was ill. Other members of Scott's "little cabinet," as his field staff became known, included Lieutenants P. G. T. Beauregard, George B. McClellan, Joseph E. Johnston, George G. Meade, and Gustavus W. Smith. Also serving with Scott's army were Ulysses S. Grant and Thomas J. Jackson. All would become either comrade or foe in the fateful years of 1861 through 1865.

Having secured a base of operations, Scott began his advance towards Mexico City on April 10, 1847. On reaching Cerro Gordo he found himself confronted by a large Mexican army commanded by General Santa Anna, who had reorganized his forces after defeat at the hands of Zachary Taylor at Buena Vista. As the Mexican positions were so formidable at Cerro Gordo, Scott had to find a means other than frontal assault. According to his report, "The reconnaissances were conducted with vigor under Captain Lee at the head of a body of pioneers, and at the end of the third day a passable way for light batteries was accomplished without alarming the enemy, giving the possibility of turning the extreme left of his line of defence and capturing his whole army." For his actions at Cerro Gordo, Lee was promoted to the rank of brevet major on April 18, 1847. On August 20 of the same year he received further promotion to lieutenant-colonel for similar brave conduct at Contreras and Churubusco.

On September 13, 1847 Lee was responsible for the positioning of the three batteries that would weaken the walls of Chapultepec Castle, which stood on a hill near Mexico City and served as a military academy for the Mexican Army. Slightly wounded later that day, he collapsed from exhaustion and loss of blood while carrying orders during the ensuing successful assault. In his official report, Scott again spoke highly of him, remarking that "Captain Lee … bore important orders from me (September 13th) until he fainted from a wound and the loss of two nights' sleep at the batteries." Years later, Scott was heard to remark that "Lee is the greatest military genius in America." For his bravery at Chapultepec, Lee received the rank of brevet colonel on the same day.

After the conclusion of the treaty negotiations with Mexico in 1848, Lee returned home with the army, and was again assigned to further duties with the Corps of Engineers. For three years, from 1849 to 1852, he was engaged in the construction of the fortifications at Baltimore, Maryland, consisting of the hexagonally shaped Fort Carroll in the Patapsco River, which was originally known as the "Fort at Soller's Point." His service there ended on September 1, 1852, on which date he was appointed superintendent at West Point, to succeed Captain Henry Brewerton. He remained in this position until April 1, 1855, during which time the course of study was extended to five years under order of the Secretary of War, dated August 28, 1854. Other improvements included the construction of a new wharf and road, and a spacious riding hall.

The acquisition of a vast area of territory that followed the war with Mexico, plus frequent fighting between Native Americans and settlers in the frontier states and territories, necessitated an increase in the size of the small regular US army during the mid-1850s. As a result, Congress passed an act authorizing the raising of two new regiments of infantry and two of cavalry, and the principal posts in these regiments were filled by selections from those officers who had most highly distinguished themselves in the war with Mexico. As a result, Lee was transferred from a staff to a line officer post and commissioned as a lieutenant-colonel of the 2nd Cavalry, which was assigned to Western Texas. The 2nd Cavalry was recruited and organized at Jefferson Barracks, Missouri, during the fall and winter of 1855–56, and marched southwest as soon as the roads were firm enough to travel. Lee left Alexandria, Virginia, to join his regiment on February 12, 1856. On arrival he was directed by his commanding officer, Colonel Albert Sidney Johnston, to proceed to Camp Cooper, on the Clear Fork of the Brazos River, which formed part of an outer chain of forts protecting the frontier, where he took command of the first and fifth squadrons of the regiment.

Lee spent the next 12 months on expedition and campaign against the marauding Comanche. This period was interrupted only by a summons to Fort Brown, on the Rio Grande, to serve on a court martial. On July 23, 1857, Johnston received orders to report in person to Washington, DC, and command of the 2nd Cavalry was turned over to Robert E. Lee. On October 21, he received news of the death of his father-in-law, George Washington Parke Custis, and promptly proceeded to Arlington for the funeral. As a result the Lees inherited Arlington House and estate.

Visiting his family at Arlington again in October 1859, and with Winfield Scott absent from the Capitol at the time, Lee suddenly found himself in command of a battalion of marines, plus two 12-pdr Dahlgren howitzers, with orders to put down an armed insurrection known subsequently as the "John Brown raid," which took place at Harper's Ferry on the 16th of that

Ordered to crush the John Brown rebellion at Harper's Ferry on October 18, 1859, future Confederate commander Lieutenant-Colonel Robert E. Lee appears here accompanied by Lieutenant "Jeb" Stuart, 1st US Cavalry. This *Harper's Weekly* engraving depicts the marines under Lee battering down the doors of the engine house that served as Brown's fort. (Anne S. K. Brown Military Collection, Brown University Library)

month. A fanatical leader of the Free Soil Party and aided by his five sons, John Brown had played a prominent part in the conflict of 1856 between free-soil and pro-slavery factions known as the Kansas–Missouri Border War. Since the suppression of that conflict, Brown had been secretly engaged in planning a slave revolt in the South. On October 16, 1859, with the aid of a party of 16 whites and five African-Americans, he "invaded" Virginia and seized the Government arsenal and other buildings at Harper's Ferry, intent on capturing the arms and handing them out to the nearby slaves who were expected to rise in rebellion.

Waiting until dawn the next day after arrival at Harper's Ferry via the Baltimore and Ohio Railroad, Lee held a council of war with his fellow officers. With hostages including local plantation owner Lewis Washington, great-grandnephew of the first president, being held by Brown, it was impossible to use the howitzers. Hence Lee decided to send Lieutenant James Ewell Brown "Jeb" Stuart, 1st Cavalry, who was serving as temporary adjutant, under a flag of truce at sunrise to attempt to persuade John Brown to surrender. If this failed, Stuart was to raise his arm as a signal, and the marines would rush the doors of the engine house. Predictably, Brown would not accept Lee's terms, which included protection and a fair trial, and the assault was begun by 24 marines led by Lieutenant Israel Greene. During the melee, John Brown was wounded by a thrust from Greene's dress sword, while all but two of his band were either killed or captured. Hauled out and laid on a mattress, Brown would later declare: "You may dispose of me very easily. I am very nearly disposed of now; but this question is still to be settled – this Negro question, I mean. The end is not yet."

"Jeb" Stuart contributed greatly to the Confederate victory at Chancellorsville in May 1863. (US National Archives 518135)

Returning to Washington, DC, with his temporary command of marines, Lee was ordered back to Charlestown, Virginia, on November 29, 1859 to take charge of security during the execution of John Brown and three of his surviving followers on December 2 and 16. Although rumor of threatened rescue attempts by abolitionists abounded, all four public hangings took place without incident.

When the lower South seceded from the Union, beginning with the secession of South Carolina on December 20, 1860, Lee began to cast what A. L. Long aptly termed as "anxious glances at the threatening aspect of the political horizon." On January 23, 1861 Lee wrote a friend: "As far as I can judge from the papers, we are between a state of anarchy and civil war. May God avert both of these evils from us!" When Texas seceded on February 19, 1861, General Twiggs surrendered all US forces in that state to Colonel Ben McCulloch, following which he resigned from the US Army and was shortly after made a Confederate general. Meanwhile, Lee returned to Washington, DC, and was appointed colonel of the 1st Cavalry on March 3, 1861, his colonelcy being signed by Abraham Lincoln, who would the following day be inaugurated as the 16th President of the United States. During the next three weeks, Lee was tormented by the possibility that he might be forced to choose between his state and his nation. During several interviews with Winfield Scott, he was advised unofficially by that elderly warrior that if he "remained with the North," he would be offered command of the Union Army with the rank of major-general. Five days after the surrender of Fort Sumter, in Charleston Harbor, South Carolina, on April 13, Lee met with Francis Preston Blair, Sr., who had founded the Republican Party in 1856 and by 1861 served as an unofficial advisor to President Lincoln. Blair asked if there was any "inducement" he could offer which might persuade Lee to "take command of the Union army?" Lee replied: "If I owned the four millions of slaves, I would cheerfully sacrifice them to the preservation of the Union, but to lift my hand against my own State and people is impossible."

On April 20, 1861, he wrote to General Scott tendering his resignation from the US army, and two days later, on the invitation of John Letcher, Governor of Virginia, travelled south to Richmond, leaving Arlington House for the last time as its owner. Finding that the convention then in session had passed the ordinance withdrawing that state from the Union, he accepted the commission of commander of "the military and naval forces" of Virginia.

Abandoned by the Lees on May 15, 1861, Arlington House and plantation was occupied by the advance guard of the Federal army nine days later. Taken by Andrew J. Russell on June 29, 1864, this photograph shows Federal troops on duty by the portico front of the house. (Library of Congress LC-B8184-10245)

THE HOURS OF DESTINY, 1861–65

Lee was greeted by cheering crowds on arrival in Richmond on April 22, 1861. He accepted his new command the next day, stating: "I devote myself to the service of my native State, in whose behalf alone will I ever again draw my sword." During the next month, he was responsible for developing an alliance with the Confederacy that permitted Confederate troops to enter the state. On May 10, he received command of all forces within her frontiers, albeit with responsibility limited to their organization, equipment and garrisoning. Meanwhile, he found himself surrounded on all sides by war. On May 24 the Federal army occupied the heights of Washington, DC, with Arlington, his former home, as headquarters for Generals Charles

Campaigns and Battles of Robert E. Lee, 1861–65

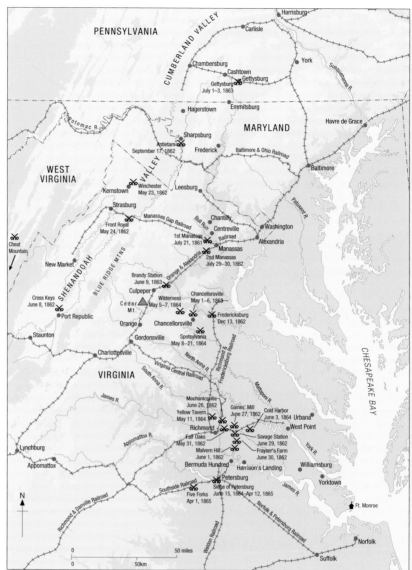

Sandford and Irwin McDowell consecutively. By then suffering from rheumatoid arthritis, his wheelchair-ridden wife would eventually be captured behind enemy lines at her son Rooney's plantation in New Kent County. A gentlemanly gesture by General George McClellan subsequently allowed her through the battle lines in order to take up residence in the beleaguered Confederate capital.

Planning his campaign for the defense of Virginia, Lee realized that the Orange and Alexandria Railroad was the quickest invasion route from Washington, DC, to the Confederate capital. This would also cut Southern communications with the Shenandoah Valley, the "bread basket" of the Confederacy. Hence, he gathered troops at Manassas Junction, which would result in the battles of First and Second Manassas in 1861 and 1862. Another possible invasion route lay up the Peninsula with Fortress Monroe as a base of operations. Alternatively, Federal troops could cross the upper Potomac River at Harper's Ferry and Williamsport, and advance into the Shenandoah Valley. Also, by forcing a passage through the mountain ranges of western Virginia, or landing a force on the sea approaches to Norfolk, Virginia, the armies of the North could threaten the safety of the South.

Thus, as fast as they arrived in Richmond and could be prepared for battle, Confederate troops were sent by Lee to these points. During this period he managed to organize and equip about 40,000 men with 115 cannon, and sent forward 114,400 rounds of ammunition, plus a million percussion caps. When ordered by Governor Letcher in April 1861 to send fellow Virginian Thomas J. Jackson to Harper's Ferry "to organize into regiments the volunteer forces which have been called into service of the state," Lee had the prescience to instruct him to dismantle and remove to Richmond the arsenal and factory arms-making machinery.

On June 8, 1861, all Virginia forces were mustered into Confederate service. Lee thus became a Confederate brigadier-general, which for several months was the most senior rank. But despite his acknowledged military reputation he was not given a field command. However, his defensive strategy placed Virginia on a strong war footing, and Lee himself would benefit when he finally took on such a responsibility in 1862. While in July 1861 the Federal Army, commanded by General Irwin McDowell, advanced towards Manassas, and Johnston and Beauregard together won the Confederate victory on the 21st of that month, Lee worked in his office at Richmond.

The Cheat Mountain campaign

On July 28, 1861 Lee was at last given a field command in northwestern Virginia. However, Davis had issued no written orders and failed to make his assignment and status clear. On July 31, the *Richmond Examiner* may have come close to the official truth when it reported that Lee was on "a tour to the West, looking after the commands of Generals Loring and Wise… His visit is understood to be one of inspection, and consultation on the plan of campaign." Certainly, Lee referred to himself as "commanding general" in Special Orders issued on September 14, and signed documents in the same manner. The lack of clarity regarding his status was to have damaging repercussions in his dealings with subordinate commanders in the ensuing campaign.

During the early weeks of the war the mountainous counties in northwestern Virginia had refused to accept the authority of the Confederate government and had welcomed the arrival of Federal troops under General George B. McClellan. Lee's orders were to coordinate a counterattack consisting of troops commanded by General William Loring, an experienced professional soldier, plus those under Henry

William Wing Loring had been an Indian fighter while Lee was a headquarters staff lieutenant, and he had seen far more field service than his commanding officer. Hence, he was reluctant to receive orders from Lee and did much to turn the Cheat Mountain campaign into a failure for the Confederacy. (Alabama Department of Archives & History – LPP00118)

15

A. Wise and John B. Floyd, both of whom were former Governors of Virginia and had been appointed only on the strength of their political background.

Lee set out for northwestern Virginia with two aides, Lieutenant-Colonel John A. Washington, great-grandnephew of George Washington, and Captain Walter H. Taylor. On arrival at Monterey, about 25 miles (40km) southwest of the Shenandoah Mountains, one Georgia soldier recalled that he was clean shaven with the exception of a heavy iron-gray moustache, and rode a dapple-gray horse, which was presumably Traveller. Meanwhile, on August 31, 1861, Lee was confirmed as a full general in the regular army of the Confederate States. Originally authorized by congress on May 16, this rank was now officially conferred.

Lee soon encountered difficulties with Loring. On July 23, General Henry R. Jackson, commanding the Monterey Division, Confederate Army of the Northwest, had ordered forward from Huntersville a reconnaissance expedition, which reported that a road from Valley Mountain descended into the Tygart's River Valley and into the rear of the Federal position in the Cheat Mountain Pass. With a stronger force, the Federals could be trapped on Cheat Mountain. However, the Northern troops quickly became aware of the situation and began to prepare fortifications farther down Tygart's Valley to prevent a Confederate advance.

Everything depended on speed if the South was to take advantage of the situation, but Loring refused Lee's request to move until he had built up a sufficient supply base at Huntersville. At this point Lee determined on diplomacy and attempted to smooth down Loring's "ruffled feathers" to win his confidence, and coax him into action when and if he could. Hence, a golden opportunity was missed and Lee had to shape a new plan of campaign in place of the one the Federals had carelessly presented, and Loring had negligently let slip by. In his dealings with Loring, Lee's reluctance to confront fellow officers showed itself for the first time. It was to manifest itself again at Second Manassas in 1862 and was to have further repercussions at Gettysburg in 1863 – with fateful consequences.

Following further Confederate failure at Cheat Mountain due to an uncoordinated attack in rough terrain and a hostile climate, Lee ordered a withdrawal to Valley Mountain on September 17, 1861. To compound matters, Colonel Washington was killed by pickets whilst reconnoitring a Union encampment at Elk Creek. During October, Lee renewed operations against Laurel Mountain with the troops of Floyd and Loring, but following another failed attack the campaign was called off.

Upon return to Richmond on October 30, 1861, the Confederate press reported that Lee was "much broken down by his arduous labours in command of the forces in the Northwest." In the atmosphere created by the victory at Manassas, his failed campaign was a great disappointment and, according to Freeman, "public expectation had outrun achievement." Although Lee regarded the whole campaign as having been a "forlorn hope" from the outset, he made no excuses and prepared no official report. Any detailed account of what had happened would of necessity have exposed the delays, mistakes, and foolish quarrels of fellow officers. His code of honor could not countenance such self-vindication, and his sense of duty to the South made him unwilling to stir up strife when unity was essential to the successful conduct of the war.

The South Atlantic coast

Davis next assigned Lee to strengthen the southern coastal defences of the Confederacy. The Carolinas had suffered Federal raids, and alarm was spreading amongst the population in other Southern seaboard regions. Describing this assignment as "another forlorn expedition" in a letter to his daughter Mildred, Lee left Richmond for Beaufort, South Carolina, on November 6, 1861. He established his headquarters at Coosawhatchie and used his Virginia experience as a guideline to organize a force of 25,000. He concentrated these troops at Charleston, Pocotaligo, and Coosawhatchie, South Carolina, and Savannah, Georgia, rather than spreading them thinly along the coast – a policy he would develop further in later campaigns. He also ordered the construction of forts and batteries beyond the range of Federal naval guns, which contained ordnance of the heaviest caliber. Obstructions were sunk in the major rivers, and extensive fortifications were begun at Savannah and Charleston, none of which was taken by sea and would only be carried via a landward assault during Sherman's march in 1864. As 1862 began there was a greater feeling of security among the people of South Carolina and Georgia than there had been felt for several months. On March 2, Lee received a telegram from Davis to return to Richmond where matters of great importance awaited his attention. Responding immediately, his remaining work on coastal defenses devolved upon General John C. Pemberton.

The Peninsula campaign

Upon arrival at the Confederate capital, Lee was given control of military operations. Retaining confidence in his general, Davis made this appointment a few weeks after the Federal capture of Fort Donelson, in Tennessee, on February 15, 1862. This was followed on March 12 by the evacuation of Winchester by Jackson in the face of the advance of McClellan, who had

Published in *Harper's Weekly*, this engraving depicts one of the bayonet charges conducted by the Federal brigade commanded by Brigadier-General Daniel Sickles during the battle of Seven Pines, or Fair Oaks, fought from May 31 through June 1, 1862. (Author's collection)

replaced McDowell following the debacle at Bull Run, and who at last had begun his long-awaited spring campaign. Waning Confederate fortunes in both the east and west clearly indicated that the Confederate War Department must have a command system adequate to control the movement of armies along the whole military frontier of the Confederacy.

By April 1862, the Northern war effort on the Virginia Peninsula had gathered pace. At McClellan's request, Lincoln had agreed that an attempt should be made to capture Richmond via that route. Since the beginning of hostilities, Fortress Monroe on the tip of the Peninsula remained in Federal hands and now it provided a valuable base of operations for McClellan's campaign. By April 4, 1862, an army of 121,500 men and 44 artillery batteries, including 70 heavy siege guns and 41 great mortars, had been landed and advanced towards Yorktown, where it met resistance from an under-strength Confederate army commanded by John Bankhead Magruder, and was forced to undertake a month-long siege before that place fell.

As commander of central and Tidewater Virginia, General Joseph E. Johnston was tasked with holding a line along the Chickahominy River, thereby shielding the Virginia Central Railroad, which was the lifeline of the Confederate capital from the Shenandoah Valley. However, he wished to abandon the Peninsula, plus the Norfolk Navy Yard, and concentrate Confederate forces around Richmond, the Carolinas, and Georgia. A subsequent thrust northwards, he believed, would threaten Washington, DC, plus Baltimore and Philadelphia beyond, and force McClellan to withdraw from the Peninsula. As a result, a crisis gripped the Confederate high command. Lee did not favour the abandonment of the Peninsula, believing that its loss, plus that of the Norfolk Navy Yard where the ironclad CSS *Virginia* was berthed, would result in the capture of Richmond. He was also concerned that there was not enough time to transfer Confederate troops northward for an assault across the Potomac River, and Federal troops under Burnside might be moved from Roanoke, on the North Carolina coast, and landed south of the James River in Virginia. Finally, Davis decided to reject Johnston's proposal, and ruled that the Peninsula line should be held.

Lee during the Cheat Mountain campaign, 1861

On September 17, 1861, the Confederate forces of the Monterey Division, Army of the Northwest, withdrew to Valley Mountain following their disappointing performance under Robert E. Lee during the Cheat Mountain campaign. A member of the 8th Tennessee Infantry wrote later that, as the weary Tennesseans and Georgians of Donelson's brigade made their way back, they passed Lee's advance headquarters and the General "'popped' upon a stump and stood erect as a cock partridge in August, and gave the passing soldiers a grand military review. He wore a black suit of corduroy goods with a broad-brimmed hat set on the side of his head, topped off with a flaming feather or cockade plume. Our men had been instructed to salute the General as they passed, but if a single man in the ranks did any such thing we did not see or hear of it… Not a voice was raised, not an old cap or hat lifted as we sullenly passed by."

As a result, Lee began to withdraw troops from the South Atlantic coast for redeployment along the Rappahannock River to prevent McDowell's corps, held at Fredericksburg to guard the Federal capital, from advancing on Richmond and taking its defenders in the rear. In the meantime, things began to worsen in the Peninsula, and Johnston evacuated Yorktown on May 4, fighting a rearguard action at Williamsburg the following day that failed to stop the Federal advance, which was only halted at Fair Oaks and Seven Pines, fought from May 31 through June 1. On the morning of the first day of battle, Lee and President Davis rode out to the headquarters of General Smith on the Nine Mile Road, where they joined Johnston. They remained there for some time during the course of the action, which became known as "a battle of strange errors" due, among other things, to the fact that General James Longstreet delayed the Confederate attack by blocking a road meant to be taken by two other divisions. Towards the end of the Confederate attack that day, Johnston was severely wounded by a stray bullet and carried from the field. As a result, Lee was assigned to the command of what would become the Army of Northern Virginia. The Confederates renewed their attack the next day, but were beaten off by reinforced and reorganized Federal troops. However, a turning point had occurred in the course of the Civil War. With this appointment, Lee at last had full license to display his extraordinary military genius.

The tide was turned in the Peninsula campaign during the Seven Days Battles fought between June 25 and July 1, when the Confederates suffered the greater losses but, because of Lee's adroit maneuvering, were able to force McClellan to retreat. Several stubborn battles – including those of Savage's Station, Frayser's Farm, and Malvern Hill – were fought, but McClellan was able to lead his troops back to the James, where he gained the support of Navy gunboats. The Peninsula campaign was a failure and the Federal army was forced to abandon the attempt to take Richmond. Meanwhile, Confederate success had bought time for Lee to regroup his army, and had given a new impetus to the Southern war effort.

Second Manassas, or Second Bull Run, 1862

Federal forces in the east were next formed into the short-lived Army of Virginia under General John Pope. McClellan was ordered to evacuate the Peninsula and join Pope, who also commanded the armies under Banks, McDowell, and Sigel. With a united army, the new Federal commander's mission was threefold – to protect Washington, DC, to defend the Shenandoah Valley, and to advance on Richmond.

Lee decided to strike first, adopting an offensive strategy that would prove very successful during the next 12 months. Marching north with an army of about 55,000 in July, 1862, he divided his force by sending 14,000 under Jackson towards Gordonsville to sweep west and north of Pope, who was still awaiting the arrival of McClellan. Jackson was subsequently reinforced by A. P. Hill's division. In early August, Pope marched south into Culpeper County, Virginia, to capture the rail junction at Gordonsville. On August 9, the Federal corps under Nathaniel Banks clashed with Jackson at Cedar Mountain. Although the Federals gained an early advantage, a Confederate counterattack led by Hill repulsed Banks' troops. The Confederate victory at Cedar Mountain took pressure off Richmond by shifting the fighting from the Peninsula to Northern Virginia.

On August 26–27, Jackson's troops destroyed Pope's supply depot at Manassas Junction, following which he moved to a position in the woods at Groveton near the old Manassas battlefield. An infuriated Pope abandoned his line along the Rappahannock and headed towards Manassas to crush Jackson. At the same time, Lee moved northward with Longstreet's corps to reunite his army. Two days later, in order to bring Pope to battle, Jackson ordered his troops to attack a Federal column as it marched along the Warrenton Turnpike. Convinced that Jackson was isolated and sure he could achieve a decisive victory before Lee and Longstreet could intervene, Pope readied his army for battle. On August 29, his army found Jackson's men posted along an unfinished railroad embankment north of the turnpike. In a series of uncoordinated attacks, which lasted throughout the afternoon, he hurled his men against the Confederates. In several places his troops momentarily breached Jackson's line, but each time they were forced back. Meanwhile, Longstreet arrived on the battlefield and, unknown to Pope, deployed on Jackson's right in order to overlap the exposed Federal left. Three times Lee urged Longstreet to attack but he declined, suggesting it would be better to make a reconnaissance that evening. For the second time since accepting a field command, Lee hesitated. His own better judgment and consideration for the opinion of a subordinate were at odds. The moment was a pivotal one in his military career, less in its effect on the outcome at Second Manassas

James "Old Pete" Longstreet's refusal to attack the Federal left flank when requested at Second Manassas on August 29, 1862 revealed for a second time a weakness in the leadership qualities of Robert E. Lee. (US National Park Service)

than in its bearing on his future relations with Longstreet. In the words of Freeman: "The seeds of much of the disaster at Gettysburg were sown in that instant – when Lee yielded to Longstreet and Longstreet discovered that he would."

The morning of August 30, 1861 passed quietly. Just before noon, mistakenly believing the Confederates were retreating, Pope ordered his army forward, but discovered that Lee stood firm. Undeterred, he ordered yet another attack against Jackson's line, which again held, and the Federals were thrown back in a bloody repulse. Observing that the Federal lines were in disarray, Longstreet at last ordered his corps to attack, rolling back the Federal left. Faced with annihilation, a rearguard action on Chinn Ridge and Henry Hill bought time for Pope's hard-pressed forces to retreat. Finally, under cover of darkness the defeated Federal army again withdrew across Bull Run towards the Washington, DC, defences. Although

Lee came close to winning a decisive victory at Second Manassas, he had allowed the Federal army to escape. However, Pope's poor qualities as a general had cost the North about 16,000 lives, while Lee lost 9,000. With little other choice, Lincoln reappointed McClellan to command the Army of the Potomac.

Regardless of various setbacks, Lee's strategy during the first three months of his command of the ANV had proved successful. Beginning in an apparently hopeless situation, with McClellan nearing Richmond from the Peninsula and other Federal forces approaching from the north, he had succeeded not only in eliminating the immediate threat, but had driven his foe back to within sight of Washington, DC.

Second Manassas, August 28–30, 1862

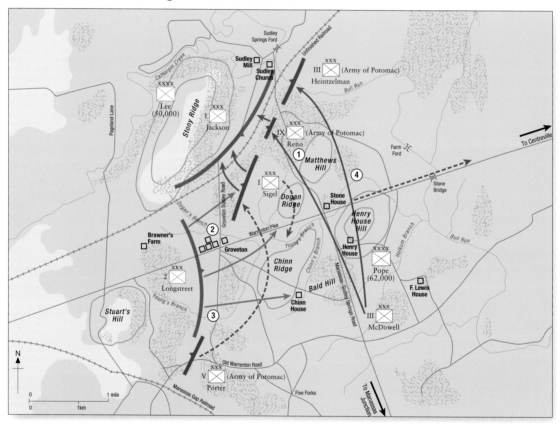

1. After two days of battle between Stony Ridge and Bull Run, Pope masses much of his army, consisting of 62,000 men, north of the Warrenton Pike on the morning of May 30, 1862.
2. As Pope's lead elements begin to storm the Confederate positions behind the railroad embankment, Longstreet at last orders his Second Corps to counterattack at 4.00pm. Anderson's Division and part of Hood's sweep forward, crossing in front of Jackson's right wing.
3. Further south, the remainder of Longstreet's troops, spearheaded by Jones' and Kemper's brigades, advances unopposed toward Chinn Ridge in a flanking movement that endangers the whole of Pope's army.
4. By 5.00pm, Pope at last realizes the danger and dispatches reinforcements from the corps of Sigel and McDowell south across the Pike towards Chinn Ridge and Henry House Hill in order to slow down the Confederate attack. This enables the bulk of the Federal army to withdraw back to the Washington, DC, defenses, and saves it from complete annihilation.

Sharpsburg, or Antietam, 1862

During September 1862 Lee invaded the North for the first time, leading 40,000 men into Maryland. In so doing he hoped to draw Federal troops from the southern coast back north in defence of Washington, DC. He also hoped to feed his army on Maryland corn, gain Maryland volunteers for the Confederate army and, by winning a decisive victory, not only demoralize the North but encourage Great Britain to recognize the Confederacy. However, Lee's invasion did not go to plan. He lost more troops by desertion and straggling than he gained by recruitment of pro-Confederate Marylanders. Also, a copy of his operational orders fell into McClellan's hands, having been discovered in an envelope wrapped around three cigars in an abandoned Confederate campsite. Discovering that Lee's army was divided, with Jackson at Harper's Ferry, McClellan was in a prime position to crush the reduced force at his front. Although he did manage to push the Confederates back toward the Potomac, Lee stood his ground behind Antietam Creek, near the township of Sharpsburg, rather than retreat back into Virginia. Considering that both his flanks were exposed and he had a wide river at his back, Lee's decision to offer battle was risky. If McClellan had attacked on September 15 or 16, Lee faced a realistic possibility of defeat. But McClellan failed to act decisively once again, allowing Jackson's "foot cavalry" to rejoin Lee's army. Although the odds were reduced, McClellan still had a two-to-one advantage when he finally attacked on September 17.

Regarded subsequently as the bloodiest single-day battle of the war, Lee lost about 10,000 men at Sharpsburg while McClellan lost 14,000 men. While the Confederate army had acquitted itself bravely, McClellan claimed victory as Lee withdrew back into Virginia on September 18. As a result, Lincoln issued the Emancipation Proclamation. Designed to free the slaves throughout the Confederacy, it would also encourage African Americans in both the North and the South to join the ranks of the Federal army to fight for their freedom. Lee's failure to achieve a decisive victory also meant there was little likelihood of British intervention on the part of the South. However, McClellan failed to follow up his success at Antietam, and an exasperated Lincoln relieved him of command on November 9, 1862, replacing him with General Ambrose Burnside.

This lithograph depicts Robert E. Lee and staff at Fredericksburg on December 13, 1862. Watching the slaughter of advancing Federal troops on Marye's Heights, Lee remarked: "It is well that war is so terrible, or we should grow too fond of it." (Library of Congress LC-USZC4-1976)

Fredericksburg, 1862

The new Federal commander shifted the area of operations to the Fredericksburg–Richmond line. Planning an offensive for late fall, Burnside intended to advance into Virginia and feint towards Culpeper before quickly marching southeast to Fredericksburg. In hopes of sidestepping Lee's army, he planned to cross the Rappahannock and approach the

A volunteer storming party, or "Forlorn Hope," of Union troops is depicted crossing the Rappahannock River at Fredericksburg on December 10, 1862, to drive off the Confederate sharpshooters who were firing on the engineers constructing the pontoon bridge seen in the rear. (Author's collection)

Confederate capital along the route of the Richmond, Fredericksburg, and Potomac Railroad. Such an operation required speed and guile. The troops under Burnside received their marching orders on November 15, and the lead elements of his army reached Falmouth, Virginia (opposite Fredericksburg), two days later having successfully stolen a march on Lee, whose army was well to the west, with Longstreet's corps at Culpeper and Jackson in the lower Shenandoah Valley.

However, Burnside was unable to capitalize on the situation as the Rappahannock was too high, and he had to wait for the arrival of pontoon bridges, which were delayed by a combination of bad weather and bureaucratic bungling. Meanwhile, Lee rushed troops to Fredericksburg and within a few days the corps of both Longstreet and Jackson deployed in virtually impregnable positions along a high ridge that curved around behind the town, with the former on Marye's Heights to the north, and the latter on Prospect Hill to the south. On December 11, 1862, Federal engineers began building six pontoon bridges opposite Fredericksburg to facilitate the crossing of the river at three points. At about 10.00am Federal cannon opened fire and about 100 guns hurled shot and shell that smashed indiscriminately into buildings occupied by Confederate sharpshooters and civilians alike.

With the bridges completed, the bulk of Burnside's forces began crossing the river and deploying for battle during the next two days, while many of his troops looted Fredericksburg. The original plan of the Federal commander was to launch the main attack against Jackson's position to the south using his Left Grand Division, with a smaller, supporting action conducted by the Right Grand Division against Marye's Heights farther north. A total of 16 unsuccessful Federal charges were made against the stone wall on Marye's Heights during the ensuing attacks on December 13.

Costing the Army of the Potomac 1,284 killed, 9,600 wounded, and 1,769 captured or missing, as opposed to only 608 killed, 4,116 wounded, and 653 captured or missing on the Confederate side, Fredericksburg was one of the most one-sided battles of the Civil War. Due to the impregnable position in which Lee had placed his troops, a mere 5,000 determined Confederates had held back an entire army. As the battle concluded, many wounded Northerners were forced to spend a freezing night on the slopes before the heights, pinned down by Confederate sharpshooters. During the afternoon of the next day, Burnside requested a truce to tend to his wounded, which Lee granted.

Having removed most of his fallen from the field, Burnside withdrew his army back across the river to Stafford Heights on December 16. Once again, Lee was pleased that he had concluded a successful campaign with another victory, but he was regretful that more had not been achieved.

During the following month, Burnside attempted to salvage his reputation by attempting to march north around Lee's left flank. However, this plan was frustrated when his troops got bogged down by January rains that reduced the roads to mud pits. Becoming known as the "Mud March," the operation was cancelled and Burnside was replaced by General Joseph Hooker on January 26, 1863.

Photographed in February 1863, this view across the Rappahannock River shows the devastated city of Fredericksburg following Lee's victory on December 13, 1862. (US National Archive photo 165-SB-30)

Fredericksburg, December 13, 1862

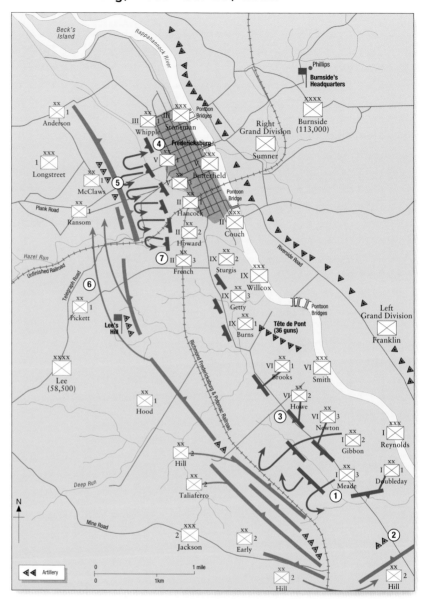

1. Burnside's main assault begins when Franklin's Left Grand Division attacks a gap in Jackson's line south of Fredericksburg in thick fog at 8.30am.

2. The Federal attack is stalled by enfilade fire from two guns of the Virginia Horse Artillery, which are placed strategically on the Confederate right flank.

3. To Meade's right, the divisions under Gibbon make better progress, but become separated from Meade's troops, and by 1.30pm a Confederate counterattack pushes them back. Eventually the divisions of Sickles and Birney are brought up to strengthen the Federal line and Jackson's advance grinds to a halt.

4. In order to draw attention away from his main attack in the south, Burnside next concentrates his attention on Marye's Heights behind Fredericksburg in the north. French's division of the Right Grand Division advances towards Confederate infantry and artillery behind a sunken road and stone wall.

5. With Franklin's main attack in the south stalled, Burnside decides to concentrate on Marye's Heights in the north. After French's division is repulsed with heavy losses, he orderes forward the divisions of Hancock and Howard, which meet a similar fate.

6. Lee orderes Pickett's Division and one of Hood's brigades north to reinforce Marye's Heights.

7. Griffin's Division renews the attack at 3.30pm, followed by Humphrey's Division at 4.00pm. Six Federal divisions are sent forward one brigade at a time, for a total of 16 individual charges, all of which fail costing Burnside about 8,000 casualties.

Chancellorsville, 1863

After Fredericksburg, Lee retained his tented headquarters midway between Fredericksburg and Hamilton Crossing, which had been chosen on account of its accessibility. Towards the end of December 1862 he dispatched cavalry to scout on the north side of the river. Towards the end of March 1863 Lee became sick and suffered a heart attack that foreshadowed his later fatal

Chancellorsville, May 2–4, 1863

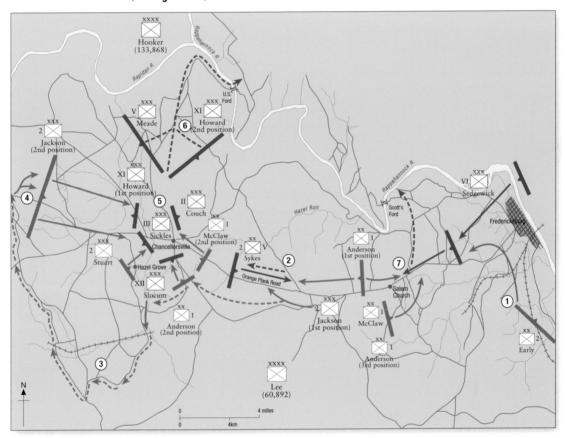

1. Leaving Early's division as a covering force at Fredericksburg, Lee marches with the remainder of the ANV to confront a Federal army over twice its size.
2. Sykes' division approaches Lee's rear along the Orange Plank Road on May 1 and encounteres fierce resistance. Sykes' troops are ordered to withdraw and concentrate at Chancellorsville, thus giving Lee the initiative.
3. On the morning of May 2, Lee sends Jackson with 26,000 men on a 14-mile (22.5km) march around the Federal right flank, leaving only 14,000 to face Hooker's army of 70,000.
4. At 5.00pm Jackson's lines surge forward in an overwhelming attack that crushes Howard's XI Corps. The Federals form a defensive perimeter around the Chancellor House.
5. Second Corps attacks and breaks through the Federal perimeter from the west at dawn on May 3. Capturing a hill called Hazel

Grove overlooking Chancellorsville, the Confederates place 30 guns there and begin pouring shot and shell into the massed Federal lines surrounding Hooker's headquarters at the Chancellor House. Meanwhile, Anderson's and McClaw's divisions under Lee close in from the southeast.
6. By noon the position of Hooker's army has become untenable and he orders it to fall back to entrenchments north of Chancellorsville prepared the night before. The Army of the Potomac finally retreats back across the Rappahannock during heavy rain on May 6.
7. Farther east, 23,000 men of the Federal VI Corps under Sedgewick manage to finally capture Marye's Heights on May 3 and advance towards Salem Church, where they are attacked on three sides by the divisions of McClaw, Anderson and Early, and escape back across the Rappahannock at Scott's Ford two days later.

illness in the post-war years. Thankfully for the Confederate cause, he was well enough to resume his duties by April 15, 1863. Near the end of that month, Hooker ordered his reorganized army of 115,000 men (consisting of II, V, XI, and XII Corps) on campaign to turn the Confederate left flank by crossing the Rappahannock and Rapidan rivers above Fredericksburg. Crossing the Rapidan via Germanna and Ely's fords, he concentrated near Chancellorsville on April 30. Sickles' III Corps was ordered to join them via United States Ford, while Sedgwick's VI Corps and Gibbon's division was retained near Fredericksburg.

Chancellorsville has been called "Lee's perfect battle" because he vanquished a much larger foe through audacious tactics. In response to Hooker's movement, he left a covering force under Jubal Early at Fredericksburg and marched with the remainder of the available ANV, amounting to just under 60,000 men, to confront a Federal army over twice its size. As the Federal division under Sykes approached Lee's rear on May 1, they encountered resistance from Anderson's division. Threatened by Jackson's flanking movement, Sykes' troops were ordered to withdraw and concentrate at Chancellorsville, thus giving Lee the initiative. On the morning of May 2, Lee took one of the greatest gambles of the war by sending Jackson with 26,000 men on a 14-mile (22.5km) march around the Federal right flank, leaving only 14,000 to face Hooker's 70,000. In position by 5.00pm, Jackson's lines surged forward in an overwhelming attack on Howard's XI Corps. However, the Federals rallied and formed a defensive perimeter around the Chancellor House, with lines extending north towards the Rappahanock. Nightfall and disorganization on both sides ended the fighting that day.

Based on a photograph of the stone wall at Marye's Heights after the battle of Fredericksburg (above), this engraving by A. C. Redwood depicts the Confederate troops of Longstreet's corps pouring their deadly fire into the advancing Federals. (Library of Congress LC-USZ62-95859/Battles & Leaders)

In the early hours of May 3, Lee instructed Stuart to take command of Second Corps following the wounding of Jackson (see below), and urged him to "Keep the troops well together and press on... work by the right wing, turning the position of the enemy so as to drive him from Chancellorsville." Lee would attack the Federal left wing at the same time. Launching a dawn attack, Stuart's corps seized the high ground at Hazel Grove, overlooking Chancellorsville, and the Confederate artillery concentrated there bombarded the Federal troops crowded around Hooker's headquarters at the Chancellor House. At this point a piece of timber concussed the Northern general, forcing him after a disastrous delay to hand over command to General Darius Couch. With one final push, Lee drove the Army of the Potomac back towards the Rappahannock where it entrenched with its back to the river near United States Ford.

After further reverses at Salem Church, Hooker's army recrossed the Rappahannock on May 4, and his campaign was over. Once again, Lee was angered that his adversaries had been permitted to slip away without being completely crushed. Turning on Dorsey Pender, one of his brigade commanders, he remarked bitterly: "You allow these people to get away!" However, repetition of a similar failure following Fredericksburg indicates a fundamental flaw in Confederate strategy for which Lee must bear some responsibility.

Although Chancellorsville is considered by many historians to be Lee's greatest victory, tragedy had struck towards the end of the second day of battle. While conducting a night reconnaissance on May 2, Jackson was wounded by friendly fire. Learning of the wounding of his most able lieutenant, Lee wrote him: "Could I have directed events, I would have chosen for the good of the country to be disabled in your stead." On receiving later word that Jackson's wounds would be fatal, he stated: "Give my affectionate regards, and tell him to make haste and get well, and come back to me as soon as he can. He has lost his left arm, but I have lost my right." Subsequent to the development of pneumonia, Jackson died of his wounds on May 10, 1863. On learning of his death, Lee is reported to have "wept a good deal," as much for his fallen comrade as for the fate of the Confederacy. He had indeed lost more than his "right arm" for, with the death of Jackson, the South lost its most effective command partnership, which had a profound effect on the rest of Lee's military career.

This lithograph by Henry A. Ogden depicts Robert E. Lee during the third day of battle at Chancellorsville. Riding his famous grey horse, Traveller, he is cheered enthusiastically by his troops as they make their final advance, which pushed the Army of the Potomac back to the Rappahannock River. (Library of Congress)

Gettysburg, 1863

Following almost a year of campaigning against the Army of the Potomac, in 1863 the opportunity again arose for Lee to strike the North. His skilful

Lee and Jackson met for the last time on the evening of May 1, 1863. The next day, Jackson was mortally wounded by friendly fire. Entitled the "Last meeting of Lee and Jackson," this lithograph by the Turnbull Brothers was produced in 1879 and is based on an original watercolor by veteran soldier John G. Fay. (Library of Congress LC-USZC4-995)

victories in the east were being undermined by waning Confederate fortunes in the western theater, with Vicksburg seriously threatened by Grant. After Chancellorsville, the Confederate administration was considering the detachment of part of Lee's army for western service. Lee's victory at Chancellorsville had been costly, as in addition to losing Jackson he had also sustained 13,000 casualties – 21 percent of his force. The transfer west of any sizable amount of troops would remove his ability to operate offensively. He would be forced to withdraw into Richmond, which he feared would

Lee at Chancellorsville, 1863

Lee's role towards the end of the third day at Chancellorsville on May 3, 1863 was described graphically by aide Charles Marshall many years later:

> General Lee accompanied the troops in person, and as they emerged from the fierce combat they had waged in 'the depths of that tangled wilderness,' driving the superior forces of the enemy before them across the open ground, he rode into their midst. The scene is one that can never be effaced from the minds of those that witnessed it. The troops were pressing forward with all the ardour and enthusiasm of combat. The white smoke of musketry fringed the front of the line of battle, while the artillery on the hills in the rear … shook the earth with its thunder and filled the air with the wild shrieks of the shells that plunged into the masses of the retreating foe… In the midst of this awful scene General Lee, mounted upon that horse [Traveller] which we all remember so well, rode to the front of his advancing battalions. His presence was the signal for one of those uncontrollable outbursts of enthusiasm which none can appreciate who have not witnessed them. One long unbroken cheer … rose above the roar of battle.

Photographed in 1863, Robert E. Lee wears his plain uniform coat with the insignia of a general officer correctly shown by three stars, the middle one being larger than the outer two, but minus the wreath prescribed by Confederate Army regulations. (Library of Congress LC-B8172-0001)

inevitably lead to a siege, starvation, and surrender. His aggressive military instinct could not permit that to happen. In his estimation, the North would eventually defeat the Confederacy by virtue of simple economics and population. Unless he took the initiative and crossed the Potomac in order to accomplish his objectives, the war could be lost.

The majority of the Confederate administration agreed with Lee, and on June 3, 1863 the ANV set out once again to invade the North, with 75,000 men from two infantry corps having been reorganized into three, with Longstreet in charge of First Corps, Richard S. Ewell commanding Jackson's old Second Corps, and A. P. Hill commanding Third Corps. Stuart's Cavalry division was augmented by six regiments and a battalion to create seven brigades. Lee moved his headquarters to Culpeper five days later, where he reviewed his entire command.

Following a clash at Brandy Station on June 9, in which Union forces under General Alfred Pleasanton were worsted by Stuart's cavalry, Lee's army advanced northwards across the Blue Ridge Mountains, and then turned northeast into the Shenandoah Valley where it headed for the Potomac once again. Setting a pace comparable to Jackson's "foot cavalry," Ewell's corps covered 50 miles (80km) in one day. As a result of Stuart's skill at screening the ANV, Ewell's troops scored a striking victory at Winchester, which, it was hoped, would set the tone for the whole campaign. Meanwhile, Hooker ordered all available Federal forces north to stand between Lee and Washington, DC.

Ewell next pushed on through Maryland into Pennsylvania, occupying Carlisle on June 27, with instructions to fan out on a three-division front in order to collect as much food as possible. Lee himself crossed the Potomac on June 25 and two days later issued General Order No. 73, enjoining his troops "to abstain, with most scrupulous care, from unnecessary or wanton injury to private property..." Unfortunately, his efforts to portray the Confederate invasion as morally superior to similar Federal operations was belied by the behavior of some Southern troops, who destroyed workshops, warehouses, mills and depots, and ransacked barns and food stores. Worst of all, some Northern free blacks were enslaved by Confederate soldiers.

Cavalry had a vital role to play in the Confederate invasion, as the location and advance of Federal forces had to be monitored carefully. To this end, Lee issued orders to Stuart on June 22, advising him to retain two brigades to guard the passes through the Blue Ridge Mountains in order to protect the Confederate rear. The remaining three brigades were to advance into Maryland and place themselves on Ewell's right flank. In a subsequent and ambiguous order issued the next day, Lee left to Stuart's discretion whether he should "pass around" Hooker's army, doing "all the

damage" it could, and eventually crossing "the [Potomac] River east of the mountains." These additional instructions were unfortunate, as many errors committed during the Gettysburg campaign stemmed from them. Lee did not intend that Stuart should conduct a full-scale cavalry raid, but required him to "move on and feel the right of Ewell's troops." The poor drafting of the second order led to a fatal misunderstanding by Stuart, whose vital cavalry force headed east on a raid through northern Virginia and Maryland. Approaching within a few miles of the Federal capital, he next rode as far north as Carlisle, Pennsylvania, remaining absent from the field of battle at Gettysburg until towards the end of the second day.

Although Stuart was missing, Lee still had sufficient cavalry to perform basic intelligence gathering, but it did not arrive in time to be of any service in the movements preceding the battle. Hence, he remained unaware that Hooker had crossed into Maryland on June 24. Stuart had observed and attempted to report the Federal II Corps en route north, but Lee failed to receive this information. Four days later, Meade replaced Hooker, whose self-confidence had never fully recovered from his defeat at Chancellorsville. Meade quickly received an accurate report on the location of the various elements of Lee's army, while Lee enjoyed no such information of Federal troop movements. Meanwhile, Lee issued orders to Longstreet's corps to follow Ewell to Harrisburg, and intended that Hill's corps should cross the Susquehanna River below that place. The Confederate advance was to continue north until Federal forces were encountered.

At approximately 10.00pm on June 29, Lee's plans were thrown into disarray when Henry T. Harrison, a civilian scout employed by Longstreet, brought word that the Army

Entitled "The Rebel Invasion of Maryland and Pennsylvania – the Rebel cavalry crossing the Potomac, June 11, 1863," this engraving was published in *Frank Leslie's Illustrated Newspaper* on July 4, 1863. (Author's collection)

Published in *Frank Leslie's* on July 11, 1863, this engraving based on an original sketch by artist George Law was entitled: "The Invasion of Pennsylvania – the rebel cavalry charging through the streets of Chambersburg, Pennsylvania, June 16, 1863." (Author's collection)

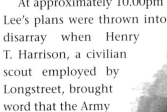

of the Potomac had crossed into Maryland, but was headed west towards the mountains. Lee concluded erroneously that the Federals were aiming for the Cumberland Mountains to cut off his communications. With Ewell still marching northeast, he determined to switch the axis of his main advance to an easterly direction in order to threaten Washington, DC, and Baltimore. Furthermore, with news that Hooker had been replaced by Meade, whom he considered overly cautious, Lee wished to bring the new Federal commander to battle as quickly as possible. Countermanding previous orders, he instructed both Ewell and Longstreet to converge on Chambersburg, which was eight miles (13km) from a small town called Gettysburg.

On June 30, the Federal 1st Division Cavalry Corps, commanded by John Buford, entered that same small town and occupied the high ground to the north and west. Unaware of this, Lee moved his headquarters to Greenwood at the western access to the Cashtown Gap of South Mountain, advising his generals that "Tomorrow, gentlemen, we will … go over to Gettysburg and see what General Meade is after." On the same day, the lead brigade of Heth's division, Hill's corps, advanced towards Gettysburg. Looking for shoes, they found Buford's cavalry, and, after a sharp engagement, the Confederates withdrew, leaving Buford to nervously await reinforcement.

July 1, 1863

On July 1, Hill ordered a reconnaissance in force towards Gettysburg of two infantry brigades, which again clashed with Buford's cavalry. As other units were drawn into combat, the fighting escalated into a general unplanned engagement. Lee had no wish to fight a full-scale battle at this stage, and gave instructions to that effect, but Hill ignored this and rashly attacked. Hearing the firing at about 11.00am, Lee is reported to have said to General Richard H. Anderson: "I cannot think what has become of Stuart… I am in ignorance as to what we have in front of us here."

Lee and staff at Gettysburg, July 2, 1863

On July 2, 1863, Lee held an impromptu council of war at his headquarters located on the western slope of Seminary Ridge, not far from the Lutheran theological seminary that gave its name to that slope. General John Bell Hood noted that Lee paced before the assembled officers, deep in thought. He also recalled that Lee halted "now and then to observe the enemy" on Cemetery Ridge with his field glasses. Despite the hot and humid weather, he wore his cadet grey frock coat "buttoned to the throat." British observer Colonel Arthur Freemantle, of the Coldstream Guards, recalled that neither Lee nor Longstreet was in the habit of carrying a side arm, and that despite Lee's martial appearance, he never seemed to wear a sword slung from his belt. Seated on the fallen tree trunk are Generals James Longstreet (1) and John Bell Hood (2), while aide-de-camp Colonel Walter H. Taylor stands at the left (3). Made by Mary Custis Lee and daughters and used from June 1862 through the summer of 1863, Lee's First National-pattern headquarters flag is held by a standard bearer at the right (4). The stars in its canton represented the Biblical Ark of the Covenant.

Richard S. Ewell's failure to act decisively on the first day at Gettysburg enabled the Federals to occupy the high ground on Cemetery Ridge and Culp's Hill and consolidate their position. (Library of Congress LC-B813- 6583)

By midday, Buford had been reinforced by Reynold's I Corps and Howard's XI Corps, and Hill's troops had been worsted and disengaged. Without word from Stuart, Lee remained reluctant to take any further fight to the Federals. At 2.30pm, he at last learned that Stuart was 30 miles (48km) away and, as a result, decided to commit himself to battle at Gettysburg. A simultaneous attack was ordered on both Federal flanks at 3.45pm. Although thrown back through Gettysburg in confusion, the Federals rallied on the high ground south of the town called Cemetery and Culp's hills. Although Lee did not have sufficient troop strength to offer support on the right, he informed Ewell that he wished him to take Cemetery Ridge "if possible." Thrown off balance by discretionary instructions from his commander and lacking what he felt was sufficient support, Ewell failed to attack. Although presented with an opportunity to seize high ground that probably offered the key to success that day, he failed to move despite the pleadings of aide Isaac Trimble, who offered to take the higher ground with a "good regiment," and who threw down his sword when his offer was rejected.

Arriving on the battlefield with his corps late that afternoon, Longstreet met with Lee on Seminary Ridge overlooking the town and counselled against a renewed attack. Expressing concern about the strength of the Federal defensive position, he recommended a strategic movement around the enemy left flank to "secure good ground between him and his capital." This would presumably compel Meade to attack a defensive position chosen by the Confederates. Feeling he had numerical superiority over the Federals for once, Lee stated in response that "If he is there tomorrow, I shall attack him," to which Longstreet is claimed to have replied: "If he is there, it will be because he is anxious that we should attack him – a good reason, in my judgement, for not doing so."

July 2, 1863

Determined to capture the ground at his front the next day, Lee's plan required Longstreet to attack the Federal left flank, while Hill's corps assaulted the center, and Ewell made a demonstration on the right. Resenting the fact that Lee had rejected his recommendation of a flanking movement, the sulking Longstreet took longer than Lee envisioned getting his corps in position. Meanwhile, Federal reinforcements continued to strengthen their position along Cemetery Ridge, and the end of their line would eventually extend to Little Round Top, one of two rocky hills nearly three-quarters of a mile (1.2km) farther south than Lee thought it was. Also, although not authorized to do so, Daniel Sickles had moved two divisions forward half a mile (800m) to slightly higher ground along the Emmitsburg Road running southwest from Gettysburg that was to have been occupied by Longstreet. In this advanced position, Sickles' troops held a salient with its apex in a peach orchard owned by farmer Joseph Sherfy, and with its left anchored in a maze of boulders known locally as "Devil's Den," just below Little Round Top. The latter development forced Lee to change his plans. He now favored extending his right until it was opposite the Round Tops, from which point he could hit the Federal left flank and roll Meade's army back. George E. Pickett's Virginia division had been delayed as it was assigned to guard Confederate lines of communication through Chambersburg, Pennsylvania.

This *Frank Leslie's* engraving illustrates the charge of Early's division, Ewell's corps, on East Cemetery Hill at Gettsyburg on July 2, 1863. (Author's collection)

With the final arrival of General Lafayette McLaws' division of Longstreet's corps, Lee asked if McLaws could redeploy his troops across the Emmitsburg Road, opposite the Federal left. In response, McLaws suggested he should reconnoiter the ground first, to which Lee agreed. Pacing up and down nearby, Longstreet intervened and ordered McLaws not to leave his division. Acting on the understanding that Lee intended a frontal assault on Cemetery Ridge, he pointed at a map and added, "I wish your division placed so," indicating a line in a direction perpendicular to that drawn by Lee. McLaws again asked if he should reconnoiter but Longstreet refused. Lee said nothing further, and a somewhat bewildered McLaws returned to his division to place it temporarily under cover. As had happened at Second Manassas in August 1862, Lee ignored insubordination from Longstreet.

The Confederate attack on the Federal left did not start until 4.30pm, when Longstreet's corps advanced, having at last been deployed by its disgruntled commander. Through a gap which lay between Sickles' left and the foot of Round Top, Hood's extreme right thrust itself unnoticed by the Federals and made a dash for Little Round Top. At this point Meade's chief engineer, General Gouverneur Warren, discovered that the smaller promontory had mistakenly been left undefended and persuaded George Sykes, commanding V Corps, to send two brigades and some artillery to that point. These troops arrived just in time to hold the summit against a furious Confederate assault. When his attack bogged down, Longstreet threw McLaws' division against Sickles' troops at the salient in the "Peach Orchard." This drove the Federal line back through a wheat field and eventually back to Cemetery Ridge, where Meade's reserves halted the Confederate onslaught. Thus, after several hours of severe fighting, Longstreet had gained the position that he could have occupied earlier in the day without resistance if he had made more haste.

Elsewhere, Hill's corps had made a strong assault against the Federal center, but Ewell's demonstration on the left, which was ordered to be made at the same time, had been delayed. It finally got underway about sunset, being conducted vigorously until after dark. For a short while Early's division managed to occupy part of Cemetery Hill, but were driven back by superior numbers. Those under Johnson also penetrated the breastworks on the extreme right of the Federal line and dug in.

According to Long, the disappointing outcome on July 2, 1863 was by no means chargeable to Lee, whose plan had been "skilfully laid, and had it been carried out in strict accordance with his instructions would probably have led to a very different result." As things stood, although Cemetery Ridge remained in Northern hands, the day's fighting had resulted in some success for the Confederates. Longstreet held the "Peach Orchard" and "Wheatfield," elements of Ewell's corps still held the breastworks on Culp's Hill, and Meade's army was believed to have received heavy casualties. As a result, there was good reason for Lee to believe that a renewed Confederate frontal attack the next day would prove successful.

July 3, 1863

The dawn of July 3, 1863 found both armies in the same position as when the battle had ended the preceding day. In order for his attack to succeed, Lee required Ewell's corps to conduct a simultaneous diversionary action from Culp's Hill, while Longstreet led the main thrust on the Confederate line. However, when Lee arrived at Longstreet's headquarters he found him still insistent on a flanking rather than frontal movement. Having had scouts confirm that Meade's right flank was still exposed and could be turned, Longstreet had already directed some of his troops to start in that direction. After listening once more to Longstreet, Lee insisted on attacking the enemy where they stood with Hood's, McLaws', and Pickett's divisions of First Corps. According to Longstreet's memoirs, he informed Lee that he had been "a soldier all his life" but "did not believe any 15,000 men could be found who would be capable of storming the ridge."

Lee's plan called for a massive assault midway along the Federal lines on Cemetery Ridge, calculating that attacks on either flank the previous two days had drawn troops away from the center. The point of attack was to be a small grove of chestnut oaks known locally as Ziegler's Grove, but described by the Confederates simply as the "little clump of trees." The attack force was to consist of Pickett's fresh division supplemented by two brigades of Pender's division under Trimble, plus Heth's division

This painting by Edwin Forbes depicts the troops of J. M. Williams' Louisiana brigade taking cover behind boulders and trees during its advance up Culp's Hill towards the breastworks on the summit. (Library of Congress LC-USZC4-1859)

of Hill's corps, by then led by Pettigrew. This provided Longstreet with a total of 11 brigades.

Meanwhile, firing began on the Federal right; Meade had determined to dislodge the Confederates under Ewell on Culp's Hill. The fighting lasted several hours, but by late morning Federal artillery had opened up and driven the Confederates from that position. Once again Lee's plans were unravelling. Regardless of this, he went ahead with the main attack. A total of 164 guns taken from all three corps, under Chief of Artillery William Pendleton, were massed in order to cover the infantry. Their concentrated fire was intended to silence and hopefully destroy all opposition.

Gettysburg: The Third Day, July 3, 1863

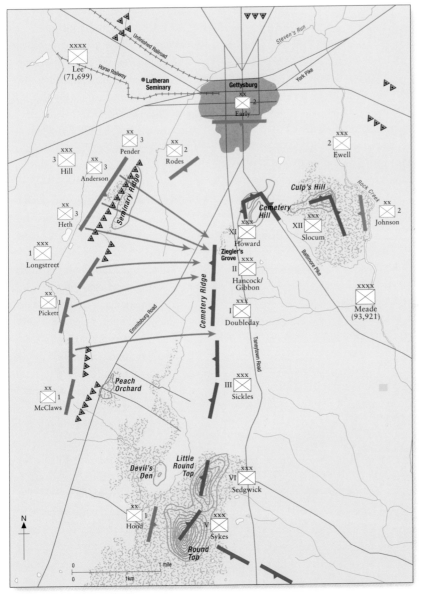

The third day of battle at Gettysburg represented a major turning point in the military fortunes of Robert E. Lee. After two days of battle, the ANV retained the initiative but the costly attacks on the Federal flanks had failed to dislodge Meade. Still determined to achieve a victory, Lee attacked the weakened Federal center on July 3, 1863. Following a two-hour bombardment that inflicted little damage on the Federal line, the Confederate infantry attack began about 3.00pm. Pickett's division advanced obliquely to their left to close ranks with Pettigrew, which exposed their right flank to Federal cannon fire. Troops under Pettigrew were similarly raked by fire. As the assault began to flounder, Federal infantry attacked its flanks. Despite dreadful losses, the Confederates broke through the lines defended by Hays' division, while the survivors of Pickett's division attacked "the angle" held by Gibbon's troops. Flooding over the stone wall to reach "the high water mark" of the Confederacy, they were driven off by Federal reserves and began streaming back to Seminary Ridge. The attack had failed and the battle was lost.

Advancing in the van, Pickett's division of 4,500 men would cause the initial breakthrough, to be followed by the six brigades of Heth and Pender, amounting to about 9,000 men, who would cut Meade's army in half. In the meantime, the remaining two brigades would serve as a reserve and flank guard. Once assured of success, Lee would throw forward Anderson's division plus a further six brigades in order to secure victory.

The bombardment began around 1.00pm and lasted for about two hours. Lee moved to the center of Seminary Ridge to observe the attack. At about 3.00pm, two wings of Confederate infantry separated by several hundred yards began to advance in two waves. However, the assault lacked artillery support as Pendleton's guns began to run low on ammunition owing to the fact that he had stationed the Reserve Artillery train too far away to sustain rapid resupply. As they converged on the "clump of trees," Lee's infantry suffered badly at the hands of Federal artillery and rifled-musket fire. To make matters worse, the main attack was not supported on the left. Having wasted its efforts against Culp's Hill, Ewell's corps failed to demonstrate against Cemetery Hill. Furthermore, although entrusted with its command, Longstreet had abdicated responsibility for the main attack and remained a passive observer. For the second time in two days, Lee had failed to coordinate his troops in order to break through Meade's solid front.

Although some Confederates temporarily broke through the Federal defences at "the angle" on Cemetery Ridge, which was ever after known as "the high water mark" of the Confederacy, what remained of Longstreet's shattered troops struggled back to their lines. As they returned to Seminary Ridge, Lee rode forward to rally their broken ranks. Lieutenant-Colonel Arthur Fremantle of the Coldstream Guards, who was on a "Grand Tour" of the South, witnessed the Confederate defeat and recorded that Lee's conduct was "perfectly sublime … and he was addressing to every soldier he met a few words of encouragement, such as, 'All this will come right in the end: we'll talk it over afterwards; but in the meantime, all good men must rally.'" Fremantle is also the main source for Lee's admission of personal responsibility for the defeat, adding that he told his men: "All this has been *my* fault – it is *I* that have lost this fight." Lee expected a Federal counterattack but none was forthcoming, which indicates the impracticality of Longstreet's suggestion to

Commanding the last Confederate troops to arrive at Gettysburg, George Pickett was immortalised in "Pickett's Charge" on July 3, 1863. (Library of Congress LC-BH83- 3754)

Lee rides among the shattered survivors of the failure of Longstreet's charge on July 3, 1863. (Author's collection)

find a better defensive position from which to encourage Meade to mount another Fredericksburg-style attack. However, having destroyed the Federal frontal assault at Fredericksburg, the ANV had now suffered the same fate at Gettysburg. Believing in the invincibility of the troops under his command, Lee had failed to acknowledge the changing face of warfare brought about by the widespread use of the rifled musket and cannon, and proof of this lay on the battlefield at Gettysburg. Avoiding further Federal attempts to crush the ANV, the Confederate retreat to Virginia began on July 4. Lee's second invasion of the North had resulted in 22,874 casualties, and had come to nought.

News of Lee's defeat filtered through the Confederacy very slowly, and was largely played down by the contemporary newspapers, which generally proclaimed the battle a draw and blamed anything else on Yankee propaganda. On July 12, 1863, a more realistic

In this print, based on a painting by Henry Alexander Ogden, George Pickett receives orders from Longstreet prior to the Confederate assault on Cemetery Ridge at Gettysburg on July 3, 1863. (Library of Congress LC-USZ62-43635)

editorial appeared in the *Richmond Examiner*, stating: "The government and its chief general undertook this campaign on their own responsibility, and at their own time. Public opinion did not impel their action… Although it has been abruptly terminated by an unsuccessful battle, we are far from thinking that the design was injudicious."

Clearly affected by such mixed criticism, Lee wrote a letter of resignation to Jefferson Davis dated August 8, 1863, in which he stated that the "remedy for want of success in a military commander" was his removal. He recommended that "a younger and abler man" be appointed in his stead. A month after receiving Lee's letter, Davis replied stating quite simply that to find an abler man was "to demand an impossibility." Indispensable to the Confederacy, Lee would remain in command for the rest of the conflict.

The Road to Appomattox

Following his failure to pursue Lee's army as it withdrew from Gettysburg, Meade planned new offensives in the fall in order to make amends. Having retreated across the Potomac to Virginia, Lee again positioned his army behind the Rapidan. In early September 1863 the Confederate commander at last sent two divisions under Longstreet to fight in Georgia. While they played a large role in the Confederate victory at Chickamauga, the move weakened Lee's own forces in Virginia. The numerical weakness of the ANV persuaded Lee of the virtues of entrenchment, which soon became part of the daily routine of campaigning. The Army of the Potomac was also reduced in strength when XI and XII Corps were sent west in

October to participate in the Chattanooga Campaign. Learning of this, Lee took the offensive again and attempted to turn the Federal flank, much as he had done at Second Manassas in August 1862. During the ensuing campaign, which was conducted from October 9 through November 9, Hill's corps was repulsed with heavy losses at Bristoe Station, while Stuart's cavalry routed Kilpatrick's cavalry division at Buckland Mills. Thus ended major operations in the eastern theater until Grant arrived in Virginia and launched the Wilderness Campaign in May 1864. With his appointment as general-in-chief of the Union armies on March 12, 1864, the Civil War entered its culminating phase.

The overland campaign, 1864

Grant's arrival in Virginia presented Lee with some challenging logistical considerations, with the corps of Ewell and Hill still in winter encampment near the Rappahannock line, and Longstreet's corps more than a day's march away at Gordonsville. Unlike his predecessors, Grant managed to keep his campaign plans out of the newspapers, and Lee found great difficulty in discerning them. Fielding an army with an effective strength of only 61,025, compared with Grant's 101,895, Lee was again at a distinct numerical disadvantage. Thus, on May 2, 1864, when he finally and correctly predicted that Grant would attempt to turn his right flank, he had difficulty in concentrating his troops to resist this move. Longstreet had to march 45 miles (72km) and did not arrive until sunrise on the second day of the battle at the Wilderness on May 6, just in time to prevent the collapse of the Confederate right flank. During this action, as Lee spurred Traveller on through the advancing Confederate ranks, the Texans of Gregg's brigade became concerned for the safety of their beloved commander and a cry of "Go back, General Lee! Go back!" was heard through the roar of battle. Following gentle persuasion from Gregg and aide Charles Venable, he finally agreed to return to his command post in the rear. Later, a devastating Confederate flank attack petered out and Longstreet was wounded in the right shoulder by friendly fire almost precisely a year after Jackson had been mortally wounded under similar circumstances only a few miles away. Tactically, the battle of the Wilderness was a draw, but Grant did not retreat as others had done before him. On May 7, he advanced his army by the left flank toward the crossroads of Spotsylvania Courthouse.

Lee's efforts to defend the northern approaches to Richmond were complicated by two other developments.

Based on a sketch by Edwin Forbes, this engraving of the cavalry battle at Yellow Tavern, which took place May 11, 1864, was published in *Frank Leslie's Illustrated Newspaper* several weeks later. With the death of "Jeb" Stuart at Yellow Tavern on May 11, 1864, Lee lost another invaluable lieutenant. (Author's collection)

Firstly, on May 9, the cavalry corps of General Philip H. Sheridan conducted a raid that disrupted Confederate lines of communication and threatened Richmond. As a result, Lee had little choice but to order Stuart to intercept him and, two days later at Yellow Tavern, Lee's dashing cavalry commander was mortally wounded by a pistol ball that entered his stomach and came out at his neck. Upon learning of Stuart's death, Lee is reported to have said that he could hardly

keep from weeping at the mere mention of his name. Secondly, Lee's army was being further drained by the campaign being conducted by Beauregard against Butler's army, which had advanced up the James River on May 5 in an additional attempt to capture Richmond. Beauregard attacked Butler at Drewry's Bluff 11 days later, forcing him to withdraw to City Point where he entrenched along the Bermuda Hundred, a tongue of land between the confluence of the James and Appomattox rivers.

Produced in 1887 by Thure De Thulstrup, this painting depicts the fighting at the Mule Shoe at Spotsylvania Court House in May 1864, during which Lee rallied his troops by riding among them. (Library of Congress – LC-USZC4-1626)

Discovering that Grant was moving towards Spotsylvania, part of Lee's forces got there first on May 9 and were deployed in a trench line that stretched for more than four miles (6.5km). However, an exposed salient known as the "Mule Shoe" (or "Bloody Angle" as it also became known) extending more than a mile in front of the main entrenchment offered Grant one major weak point to exploit on May 10 and 12. On the first date, 12 Federal regiments under the command of Colonel Emory Upton broke through the Mule Shoe along a narrow front. Lacking support, they were pushed back by nightfall. In heavy rain and thick fog on the second day of attack, Lee mistakenly thought Grant was withdrawing and moved most of his artillery from the salient in preparation for pursuit, only to learn that the Federal II Corps had broken through the Mule Shoe. During both of these onslaughts, Lee again entered the thick of the fighting to rally his shattered troops. On the latter occasion, chants of "Lee to the rear" from the ranks finally persuaded him to resort to a safer location, but only after his path had been blocked by General John B. Gordon and members of his staff, to which he replied: "If you will promise me to drive these people back from our works, I will go back." The battle in the Mule Shoe lasted for an entire day and night, as the Confederates slowly won back most of the ground they had lost, inflicting heavy losses on the Federals in the process.

After a repulse by Confederate artillery on May 18, Grant marched his vast army east and south. However, Lee forced it apart at North Anna Creek by deploying his own force in an inverted "V," and on May 26, as Grant advanced toward Richmond, Lee formed a strong defensive line along

Totopotomoy Creek. On May 30, Lee attacked part of Grant's army near Bethesda Church, and on June 1 the armies clashed in the battle of Cold Harbor. Three days later, Grant launched a frontal attack to break Lee's line but was repulsed, with 12,000 Northern soldiers killed or wounded. Strategically the overland campaign, which ended after the slaughter at Cold Harbor, was a Federal success as Grant's army was only about six miles (9.7km) from Richmond. But it had cost 60,000 Northern casualties, plus perhaps 35,000 Confederate losses, and Richmond was still in Confederate hands.

Petersburg, 1864–65

Having failed to break through at Cold Harbor, Grant decided to change his strategy. Instead of confronting and defeating Lee's army north of Richmond, he would capture the Confederate capital by crossing the James and approaching from the south. By cutting the Confederate supply lines and capturing Petersburg with his larger army and superior resources, he believed he could either starve the ANV into submission or lure them away from Richmond for a final, decisive battle.

With the assault on Petersburg, Lee was forced into a largely defensive strategy. Under the immediate command of Beauregard until October, the 5,400 defenders of Petersburg were driven from their first line of entrenchments back to Harrison Creek. Meanwhile Beauregard stripped the Howlett Line in the Bermuda Hundred to defend the city, and Lee rushed reinforcements from the ANV. On June 18, the Federals attacked again but were repulsed with heavy casualties. By now the Confederate defences were sufficiently manned and the greatest opportunity to capture Petersburg without a siege had been lost.

In the meantime, Lee appointed Ewell to command the Richmond defences, and placed Second Corps, often styled "the Army of the Valley," under Early. Persuading Davis that Confederate strategy should still be "to draw the attention of the enemy to his own territory," he authorized Early to invade Maryland and, if possible, threaten Washington, DC, to take pressure off Petersburg. Receiving Lee's usual instruction to be guided by "good judgement," Early set off on June 13, 1864. Achieving victory at both Lynchburg, Virginia, and Monocacy, Maryland, he managed to approach within five miles (8km) of the Federal capital, but Northern reinforcements prevented him from penetrating the Washington, DC, defences.

On the Petersburg front, a Federal siege-mining operation culminated in the battle of the Crater on July 30, 1864. When the mine was exploded under Elliott's Salient it blew a crater

Nicknamed "Little Billy" because of his diminutive stature, William Mahone was tasked with closing the gap in the Petersburg defences caused by the mine explosion on July 30, 1864. (US National Archives NWDNS-111-B-5123)

170ft (52m) long, 60ft (18m) wide and about 30ft (9m) deep, killing and wounding at least 278 Confederates. Fortunately for Lee, the Federals failed to take advantage of the breach and Lee ordered Mahone's brigade to cover the gap. A Confederate charge drove the enemy back to their own lines at a cost of 3,798 Federals killed, wounded and missing. Overall Confederate casualties probably amounted to about 1,500.

By the end of the summer of 1864 Lee had failed to break Grant's grip on Petersburg and Richmond. Although he had managed to keep his lines of communication open with Wilmington, North Carolina, his sole surviving port, his defence works stretched for 35 miles (56km) and were manned by an army outnumbered by almost three to one. Grant continued to make probing attacks and the Confederates lost Fort Harrison in front of Richmond at the end of September, but repelled an attack on the Boydton Plank Road to the southwest a month later. As winter descended both armies settled into an artillery duel in which Grant had the advantage. A massive 13in. mortar nicknamed "the Dictator" inflicted great psychological, if little physical, damage to the inhabitants of Petersburg.

By February 1865, Lee's dwindling army continued to deal harsh punishment to any Federal attack. But on February 22, Lee confided to Longstreet that should Sherman continue to march through North Carolina, link up with the army of John M. Schofield, which had captured Wilmington, and then drive further north, Richmond would have to be abandoned. In order to avoid such a calamity, he had no choice but to attempt a counterattack on the siege lines east of Petersburg in an attempt to deter Grant from extending his works any further westward. It was also hoped that a Confederate breakout might enable a link-up with Johnston's army in North Carolina. He entrusted the operation to Gordon, who selected as his objective Fort Stedman, which was only 300 yards from the Confederate defences and one of the weakest points on the Federal lines. Attacking at dawn on March 25, 1865, 18,000 Confederates spearheaded by axmen and storming parties completely surprised the enemy and captured the fort, but soon lost it in a Federal counterattack. Lee's last offensive had failed.

Attempting to break out of the Petersburg siege lines, General John B. Gordon was entrusted with the attack on Fort Stedman on March 25, 1865, which represented Lee's last offensive of the Civil War. (US National Archives NWDNS-111-B-1786)

Confederate collapse, 1865

Phil Sheridan arrived outside Petersburg on March 26, 1865, having defeated the remaining Confederates in the Shenandoah Valley. Grant sent Warren's corps to occupy the Boydton Plank Road on Lee's far western flank three days later, while ordering Sheridan even farther west toward Dinwiddie Court House. In response, Lee ordered Pickett to make every effort to prevent the Southside Railroad from being cut. After a fierce fight near Lewis Farm, Pickett was forced to withdraw to trenches along the White Oak Road, with its center resting on a crossroads called Five Forks. Aware of possible impending disaster, Lee sent Pickett a dispatch stating: "Hold Five Forks at all hazards." Attacking on April 1, 1865, Sheridan rolled back the Confederate left flank, while Pickett

Opposite: Serving with Caskie's Battery of Artillery during the siege of Petersburg, John Elder portrayed the charge of Mahone's brigade on The Crater in this oil painting produced in 1869. (Battles & Leaders)

enjoyed a shad fish bake several miles behind the lines, where he remained unaware of developments due to an acoustic shadow until it was too late. With Pickett's line smashed and the Southside Railroad captured, Grant ordered a general assault on Petersburg. As shot and shell crashed around his headquarters at Edge Hill, Lee telegraphed Richmond: "It is absolutely necessary that we should abandon our position tonight, as we run the risk of being cut off in the morning."

Above: This depiction of the stacking-of-arms ceremony on April 12, 1865 was produced by *Harper's Weekly* artist John R. Chapin. (Courtesy of the Appomattox Court House National Historical Park)

As soon as Grant became aware of the Confederate collapse, he ordered forward his whole available force of about 80,000 men. With Richmond ablaze, Lee hurried westward towards Danville, where he could move his army by train to North Carolina to join Johnston, who was harassing Sherman's advance north. Meanwhile, on April 3 Mayor Joseph Mayo surrendered Richmond to the Federal commander in its vicinity, and General Godfrey Weitzel took immediate possession of the city.

Below: The last council of war of the leaders of the ANV took place at Lee's headquarters on April 8, 1865. Present were James Longstreet, John B. Gordon, and Fitzhugh Lee. (Courtesy of the Appomattox Court House National Historical Park)

Lee hoped to find supplies waiting at Amelia Court House, but an administrative error meant none were there. Hence, the survival of his army was dependent on foraging for what little food remained in the countryside. By April 6, Sheridan's cavalry was on Lee's flank with infantry following closely behind. While bringing up the rear Ewell's entire corps (amounting to about 10,000 men) was surrounded and captured at Saylor's Creek. What remained of the shattered ANV continued its retreat and reached Farmville on April 7, where each man received two days' rations and a short rest. On the same day, some "principal officers" communicated to Lee their feeling that "the contest should be terminated and negotiations opened for a surrender of the army." According to Pendleton, "General Lee was lying on the ground... He received my communication

with the reply, 'Oh no, I trust it has not come to that... we have yet too many bold men to think of laying down our arms.'" Nonetheless, a correspondence was opened with Grant, beginning with a message from the Federal commander pointing out "the hopelessness of further resistance." Lee replied asking what the terms of surrender might be, and Grant responded that all officers and men would be disqualified from "taking up arms against the Government of the United States until properly exchanged."

Regardless of these negotiations, Lee continued his retreat, making better progress on April 8, but hopes of finding more supplies at Appomattox Court House were dashed when he discovered on arrival that they had been captured. Despite being virtually surrounded, and facing overwhelming odds, he determined to make one more effort to fight his way through, and that evening held the last council of the leaders of the ANV. Present were Longstreet, Gordon, and Fitzhugh Lee, and it was decided that a breakout the next morning might still be possible if Federal cavalry were the only troops found to their front.

At 3.00am on April 9, 1865, Gordon advanced what remained of Second Corps plus 30 pieces of artillery to the heights above Appomattox Court House, to discover that the route was indeed blocked by a large force of Federal cavalry. Some well-directed shells together with a cavalry charge dispersed them, but Gordon's troops encountered overwhelming numbers of Federal infantry. Without further reserves, and Longstreet's corps occupied with holding Meade back in the rear, Lee was unable to respond to Gordon's request for reinforcements, and at last accepted that it was time to suspend hostilities and arrange terms of surrender. Rejecting suggestions that the ANV should disperse and resort to guerrilla warfare, he turned to his aide Charles Venable, stating: "Then there is nothing left me but to go and see General Grant, and I would rather die a thousand deaths."

Fitzhugh Lee led the last Confederate charge near Appomattox Court House, Virginia, on April 9, 1865. (Photographic History of the Civil War)

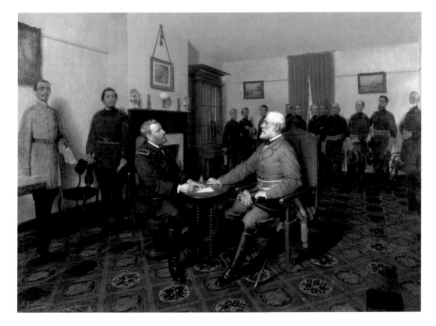

The well-known depiction of Robert E. Lee's surrender of the Army of Northern Virginia, painted by Louis Guillaume (1816–92) in 1874. (Courtesy of the Appomattox Court House National Historical Park)

An improvised flag of truce was carried to Grant, requesting a ceasefire. Meanwhile, the Confederate artillery was withdrawn from the heights and parked in a small valley to the east of Appomattox Court House while the infantry stacked arms close by. Accompanied only by aide Charles Marshall, Lee met Grant at 11.00am at the residence of Wilmer McLean, who had actually moved to Appomattox from Manassas in 1863 to avoid further exposure to battle. After exchanging courtesies, the terms of the surrender, which were the same as Grant offered at Vicksburg in 1863, were written out. They required rolls to be made of all Confederate officers and men. All arms, artillery, and public property was to be surrendered, although officers were permitted to retain side arms, private horses, and baggage. Lastly, every member of the ANV who owned a horse or mule was allowed to retain it for farming purposes. Lee remarked that the latter would have "a happy effect." He also requested rations for 25,000 men, who had been living on nothing but parched corn for several days. These were supplied from the carloads of Confederate provisions captured by Federal cavalry. With the negotiations completed, Lee returned to his shattered army to bid it farewell. Meeting Grant again on April 10, the Federal commander tried to persuade Lee to surrender the three remaining Confederate armies, as he had only surrendered the ANV, but Lee declined. They also discussed the condition of the country, and then went their separate ways.

Based on his first encounter with Lee in the Cheat Mountain campaign in northwestern Virginia in 1861, George Brinton McClellan (1826–85) believed that Lee was "too cautious and weak" and "timid and irresolute in action." His defeat during the Seven Days' battles in 1862 taught him otherwise. (US National Archives 111-B-4624)

OPPOSING COMMANDERS

McClellan

In comparison with Lee, George B. McClellan was overly cautious and concentrated too much on his own political ambition of becoming a Democratic President of the US. Meanwhile, Lee left politics to Jefferson Davis and got on with defending the Confederate cause. In a letter to Lincoln several months before Lee suddenly replaced Joseph Johnston in command of the Confederate army in Northern Virginia, McClellan stated that he thought Lee would be an easier opponent than his predecessor, remarking that he was "too cautious and weak under grave responsibility – personally brave and energetic to a fault, he is yet wanting in moral firmness when pressed by heavy responsibility, and … likely to be timid and irresolute in action." Based on Lee's performance in northwestern Virginia, McClellan might have been justified in holding this view, but quickly learned otherwise during the Peninsula Campaign of 1862.

McClellan graduated from West Point in 1846 and served with distinction in the Mexican War. He later worked on various engineering projects, including the survey for a Northern Pacific Railroad route across the Cascade Range from 1853 to 1854. Resigning from the army in 1857, he worked as a railroad official until the outbreak of the Civil War. In May 1861, he was appointed commander of the Department of the Ohio and a major-general in the regular army. His success at Rich Mountain just ten days before the Federal disaster at Bull Run placed him squarely in the public eye at a critical time. Given command of the troops in and around Washington, DC, in November he replaced the aged Winfield Scott as general-in-chief. Reflecting public opinion, the Lincoln administration pressed for an early offensive, but McClellan insisted on adequate training and equipment for his army. In March 1862, he was relieved of his supreme command, but he retained responsibility for the Army of the Potomac, with which he initiated the Peninsular Campaign in April 1862.

The collapse of this campaign after the Seven Days' battles was blamed by many on his being overly cautious. In August 1862 most of McClellan's troops were reassigned to the Army of Virginia under John Pope. After Pope's defeat at Second Bull Run, McClellan was again placed in command of Union forces, and during the Antietam campaign he checked Lee's first invasion of the North. Slow to pursue him across the Potomac, he was again removed from command in November 1862.

John Pope (1822–92) was born in Louisville, Kentucky. Aggressive in his campaign planning in 1862, he was completely outwitted by the strategy of Lee and the tactics of Jackson at Second Bull Run. (Library of Congress LC-B813- 2136 A)

Pope

Condoning the destruction of Southern property, and issuing General Order No. 5 on July 18, 1862 announcing that his army "will subsist upon the country," John Pope quickly earned the disrespect of Lee, who actively desired to humiliate his Northern opponent. Pope was born in Louisville, Kentucky, on March 16, 1822. Entering West Point at the age of 16, he graduated 17th in a class of 56 in 1842 and was assigned to the Topographical Engineers. During the Mexican War he fought under Zachary Taylor at Monterrey and Buena Vista, for which he was appointed a brevet first lieutenant and captain respectively.

In July 1861, Pope was appointed a brigadier-general of volunteers, and by 1862 commanded the Army of the Mississippi, gaining victories at New Madrid and Island Number 10. On March 21, 1862 he was promoted to major-general and transferred to the Eastern Theater where he was appointed to command the new Army of Virginia. On July 14, 1862, he alienated his own troops by issuing an address in which he declared his desire to show eastern soldiers how a western general fought, with statements such as:

"Let us understand each other. I have come to you from the West, where we have always seen the backs of our enemies… I presume that I have been called here to pursue the same system and to lead you against the enemy. It is my purpose to do so, and that speedily." Pope thus made a bad situation even worse by offending the sensibilities of his own men, who were long accustomed to defeat.

Furthermore, in pursuit of promotion, he antagonized his fellow officers who thought him pompous, abrasive, and intolerant. When asked by a reporter where his headquarters would be, he replied "in the saddle," which prompted the quip that Pope had his headquarters where his hindquarters should have been. He favoured a hard war against the Confederacy, whereas McClellan and other conservative generals sought to limit the destruction of Southern economy and society. Wrongly dismissed by many as incompetent, Pope's abilities as a general initially appeared energetic and well considered. His planning at the beginning of the Second Bull Run Campaign was effective, and it was only when faced with the strategy of Lee and the tactics of Jackson that he lost complete control of events and witnessed his short-lived army beaten, but not routed.

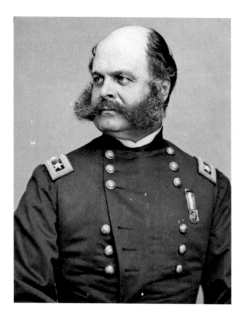

Ambrose Burnside (1824–81) rose to Civil War fame due to his successful operation on the North Carolina coast, but was responsible for Federal failure at Fredericksburg in 1862 and the mine assault at Petersburg in 1864. (Library of Congress LC-B813-1625 A)

Biographer John Cozzens argues that behind the public *braggadocio*, Pope cracked under the pressure caused by the recent death of his daughter and the awesome responsibilities of commanding an army, stating that he "buried his fears with wishful thinking, hid his errors by distorting the truth, and obfuscated the rest with gasconade." Hoping to have cornered the elusive Jackson, he wished away the rest of Lee's army, leaving himself open to a devastating Confederate counterattack. Withdrawing his troops in an orderly fashion back into the Washington, DC, defences, he blamed the defeat on officers loyal to McClellan. Although Lincoln apparently agreed, he stated that there was "an army prejudice against him, and it was necessary he should leave." Pope also blamed his defeat on Fitz John Porter's failure to carry out orders to attack on the first day of fighting at Second Manassas, and, at Pope's behest, Porter was court-martialled. Pope was relieved of command on September 2, 1862 and replaced by McClellan. He remained on active duty and commanded the Department of the Northwest for much of the rest of the war.

Burnside

Accepting command of the Army of the Potomac only at the urging of fellow officers who did not want to serve under the bombastic Hooker, Ambrose E. Burnside was placed under considerable pressure by Lincoln to take aggressive action when appointed in November 1862. Burnside had resigned his regular army commission in 1853, after graduating from West Point in 1847 and serving in the Mexican War and the Army of the Frontier. With the onset of Civil War, Burnside was appointed colonel of the

1st Rhode Island Detached Militia and commanded a brigade at First Bull Run, following which he was promoted to brigadier-general. He next led a successful expedition against the Confederate coastal installations of North Carolina, and gained further promotion to major-general. Following this, he twice refused an offer to command the Army of the Potomac. His undistinguished leadership of IX Corps at Sharpsburg, or Antietam, greatly contributed to the Federal failure to break through Lee's lines. Having been given command of the "Right Wing" of the Army, consisting of I and IX Corps, McClellan separated these two corps, placing them on opposite ends of the Federal battle line, with Burnside in immediate command of IX Corps only. As a result, Burnside responded only slowly to McClellan's orders when required to take the Rohrbach Bridge. Furthermore, failing to perform adequate reconnaissance of the area, he did not take advantage of several convenient fording sites out of range of the enemy, and his troops were forced into repeated assaults across a narrow bridge that was dominated by Confederate sharpshooters on high ground.

Despite this poor performance, he was offered and finally accepted command of the Army of the Potomac on November 7, 1862. Although presented with the opportunity to split Lee's separated army in two and defeat them in detail, he refused to allow Sumner's "Right Grand Division" to cross the Rappahannock, giving Lee time to gather his forces at Fredericksburg. His subsequent failure at that place on December 13, for which he publicly admitted blame, led to demotion to command of the Army of the Ohio, a responsibility he held until December 12, 1863. Returning east as commander of IX Corps, he fought in the overland campaign, but was again relieved of command for mishandling the Petersburg mine assault on July 30, 1864.

Hooker

Nicknamed "Fighting Joe" Hooker due to a clerical error as a result of Federal newspaper reports entitled "Fighting – Joe Hooker," Major-General Joseph Hooker was quoted by a *New York Times* army correspondent as saying shortly before he was appointed commander of the Army of the Potomac: "Nothing would go right until we had a dictator, and the sooner the better." One of the most immodest and immoral of the Federal commanders to oppose Lee, Massachusetts-born Hooker was a West Pointer who had been posted to the artillery but was serving as a staff officer when he won three brevets in the Mexican War. Unfortunately for his later career he testified against Winfield Scott before a court of inquiry on the Mexican War, and after a two-year leave resigned on February 21, 1853, to settle in California where he went into farming and the land business.

At the outset of the Civil War, Hooker was appointed a colonel of the California militia. However, he promptly offered his services to Washington but was initially rejected,

Appointed to command on January 26, 1863, the pompous Joseph Hooker (1814–79) announced that the Rebel army was "the legitimate property of the Army of the Potomac" shortly before he was completely out-fought by Lee at Chancellorsville in May of that year. (Library of Congress – DIG-ppmsca-19395)

possibly due to his anti-Scott testimony. Appointed a brigadier-general on May 17, 1861, he commanded a division of III Corps from Yorktown through Second Bull Run and Chantilly in 1862. Promoted to major-general on May 5, 1862, he led I Corps, Army of the Potomac, at South Mountain and Antietam, where he was wounded in the foot. Next given command of the Center Grand Division at Fredericksburg, he derided Burnside's plan to assault the fortified heights behind the city, deeming them "preposterous." His Grand Division and particularly V Corps suffered serious losses in 14 futile assaults ordered by Burnside despite Hooker's protests. Following up this battle with the humiliating "Mud March" in January 1863, Burnside received further criticism from Hooker that bordered on formal insubordination. As a result, Burnside planned a wholesale purge of his subordinates, including Hooker, and drafted an order for Lincoln's approval stating that Hooker was "unfit to hold an important commission during a crisis like the present." But the president's patience had run out once again and he removed Burnside instead, naming Hooker as the commander of the Army of the Potomac on January 26, 1863. During the spring of 1863, Hooker reorganized and retrained the Army of the Potomac and announced, "I have the finest army on the planet. I have the finest army the sun ever shone on… If the enemy does not run, God help them. May God have mercy on General Lee, for I will have none."

Lee had no intention of retreating at Chancellorsville, despite facing an army twice the size of his own. By dividing his forces and permitting Jackson to march the bulk of his army west across the front of the Federal line unnoticed to a position opposite its exposed right flank, he took Hooker completely by surprise towards the end of the second day of battle. Hooker's failure at Chancellorsville can also be attributed to his being knocked senseless by a Federal cannonball that smashed a wooden post into him at the Chancellor House. Rendered unfit for command at a critical moment in the battle, he only reluctantly turned responsibility over to his second-in-command, General Darius N. Couch. Relieved of command on June 28, 1863, he was given the Thanks of Congress for defending Washington, DC, and Baltimore, being one of only 15 officers to receive this honor during the war. He continued to serve in the regular army until retirement in 1868.

Meade

A captain in the Corps of Topographical Engineers before the Civil War, George G. Meade was promoted to brigadier-general of volunteers on August 31, 1861, based on the recommendation of Pennsylvania Governor Andrew Curtin. He was severely wounded at White Oak Swamp in 1862, but recovered sufficiently to take part at Second Bull Run, commanding a brigade of Pennsylvanians in McDowell's III Corps of the Army of Virginia. His brigade made a heroic stand on Henry House Hill to protect the

Although George Meade (1815–72) commanded respect from Lee and successfully resisted all Confederate efforts to break through during the three days at Gettysburg, he allowed Lee's army to slip back across the Potomac and was completely outmaneuvered in both the Bristoe and Mine Run campaigns later in 1863.
(US National Archives NWDNS-111-B-3298)

retreating Federal Army, as a result of which he rose rapidly through the ranks, distinguishing himself at South Mountain on September 14, 1862, commanding the 3rd Division of I Corps, Army of the Potomac. At Antietam four days later, Meade replaced the wounded Hooker in command of I Corps, but was again wounded. During the Federal attack at Fredericksburg in December 1862, Meade's division achieved the only breakthrough, but he failed to reinforce his success, leading to the loss of much of his division. Nonetheless, he was promoted to major-general and received command of V Corps, which he led at Chancellorsville during the spring of 1863. Meade replaced Hooker as commander of the Army of the Potomac on June 28, 1863. According to A. L. Long, Lee was surprised to learn of the change of Federal commanders at such a critical stage, and considered it "advantageous to the Federal cause as he had always held Meade in much higher estimation as a commander than Hooker."

Although he showed remarkable courage by accepting battle with Lee at Gettysburg only two days after his appointment, Meade failed to pursue the Confederates during their retreat, and was completely outmaneuvered by Lee in both the Bristoe and Mine Run campaigns. With the appointment of Grant as general-in-chief of the Union armies on March 12, 1864, Meade felt passed over and offered to resign. Refusing to accept his resignation, Grant established his headquarters with Meade, which caused additional friction between them for the remainder of the war.

Ulysses S. Grant (1822–85) eventually became the 18th President of the United States. (Library of Congress LC-USZ61-903)

Grant

By far the most formidable of Lee's opponents, Ulysses S. Grant was an excellent strategist who understood that the North had a huge advantage over the South in terms of manpower and in manufacturing capabilities. He possessed a quiet modesty combined with a determination to keep "moving on" until the war was won. He enjoyed a considerable numerical advantage over Lee in 1864, fielding 95,583 infantry, 15,298 cavalry, 8,000 artillerymen, and 274 guns. Furthermore, his appointment as general-in-chief left him free to concentrate on the main thrust and direction of the campaign, while most duties relating to command of troops in the field were delegated to Meade. When asked by an Ohio chaplain in April 1865 what he thought of Grant, Lee ascribed to him the possession of "the noblest attributes of American manhood," and that he had "all the requisites and talents for the organization of armies."

A regimental quartermaster with the rank of captain during the Mexican War, Grant was

Drawn by Alfred Waud, this sketch depicts Lee leaving the McLean House following his surrender to Ulysses S. Grant on April 9, 1865. (Library of Congress – LC-DIG-ppmsca-21320)

awarded two citations for gallantry and one for meritorious conduct. After the war he was unable to adapt to the monotony and isolation of military service on the West Coast. He drank heavily, thereby neglecting his duties, and eventually resigned from the army in 1854 to avoid court-martial. Settling in Missouri, he became increasingly destitute as he failed to make a success of various business ventures. With the outbreak of the Civil War he offered his services to Governor Richard Yates and trained recruits at Springfield, Illinois. He accepted the colonelcy of the 21st Illinois Infantry in June 1861, and in August was appointed brigadier-general of volunteers commanding the critical District of Southeast Missouri with headquarters at Cairo, Illinois. Following an unspectacular action against Confederate-occupied Belmont, Missouri, on November 7, 1861, he captured national attention after victories at Forts Henry and Donelson, Fort Shiloh in 1862, and at Vicksburg in 1863. His willingness to fight and ability to win impressed Lincoln, despite rumours of his continued inebriation. As a result, Grant was appointed General-in-Chief of the Armies of the United States, with the rank of lieutenant-general in the regular army, on March 12, 1864. Reauthorized by US Congress with Grant in mind, this rank had not been awarded since 1775 when George Washington was appointed commander-in-chief of the Continental Army, although Winfield Scott had received the brevet rank in 1855. Summoned east to Washington, DC, Grant planned and implemented the overland campaign to capture Petersburg and Richmond, Virginia, and finally forced Lee to surrender at Appomattox Court House on April 9, 1865. Following that fateful meeting with the Confederate commander, Grant stated that he felt "sad and depressed at the downfall of a foe who had fought so long and valiantly, and had suffered so much for a cause, though that cause was," he believed, "one of the worst for which a people ever fought."

INSIDE THE MIND

At the heart of the strategy and tactics employed in battle by Lee were the *Principles of War* as proposed by Carl von Clausewitz and demonstrated by Napoleon Bonaparte between 1799 and 1815. This was interpreted by Swiss military theorist Baron Antoine Henri de Jomini, who explained the Napoleonic method of warfare in his book *The Art of War*, published in 1838. Such works were studied assiduously by Lee, and used to brilliant effect by him during the Civil War. For example, at Second Manassas in August 1862 he ordered Jackson to place his corps in what Jomini termed a "strategic front" along an unfinished railroad embankment to fight and wear down Pope's army. Meanwhile, Longstreet's arriving troops were ordered to attack the exposed Federal left flank, which they eventually did with devastating effect. At Chancellorsville in 1863, Lee employed a classic Jomini-style "strategic envelopment," or turning movement, by sending Jackson's corps on a 14-mile (22.5km) march around the Federal right flank, which resulted in the decisive collapse of Hooker's army and yet another victory for the Confederacy. Yet Lee was also capable of misjudgement, as on the third day at Gettysburg when he ordered a frontal assault on the Federal center. Although possibly due to the effects of fatigue following his heart attack, such a decision failed to fully take into account developments in weapons technology and field fortifications. As a result, his infantry was cut to pieces by rifled-cannon and rifled-musket fire as it advanced vainly across open country towards Meade's breastworks along Cemetery Ridge.

On a personal level, the traditional view of Lee as an icon of military leadership is somewhat challenged today by a greater understanding of his difficult childhood and the impact it had on his later military career. Born into the Lee and Carter families, who had been leaders in the colonial government of Virginia, Robert's grandfathers both signed the Declaration of

Less than a week after his surrender at Appomattox Court House, Robert E. Lee was photographed by Matthew Brady in front of the back door of his home in Richmond. A long-time acquaintance of Lee, Brady persuaded him to pose, as historian Douglas Southhall Freeman remarked, before "the fire of battle had faded from his eyes." (Library of Congress LC-BH831 – 563)

Independence. His father, Harry Lee, had fought under George Washington during the Revolutionary War, and had served three terms as governor of Virginia. However, the family reputation of the Lees was besmirched by the financial ruin of his father. As a result, young Robert grew up surrounded by very challenging circumstances in which he also had to care for his ailing mother on a daily basis. This undoubtedly made him excessively self-disciplined and liable to accept discomfort to the extent that any sense of joy or pleasure might be perceived as improper. Throughout his entire life he never used tobacco, although he did enjoy an occasional glass of wine. While he appears never to have commented on the drinking history of Grant, the intemperate habits of many under his command were, according to Armistead Long, "always a source of pain to him," and on several occasions he quietly reprimanded "young men who had over-indulged in strong liquor." Lee was also very frugal in his approach to campaign life throughout the Civil War. Always leaving as many men as possible available for line duty, he had an undermanned staff, travelled with a minimum of baggage, and used a dinner service of tin, which served him until after Appomattox.

Another possible impact of Lee's personal life and unhappy upbringing was his strong desire to avoid any form of personal confrontation. This trait had disastrous consequences when dealing with some fellow officers during the Civil War. Biographer Roy Blount, Jr. assesses Lee as a man of competing impulses: "One of the greatest military commanders in history," who was nonetheless "not good at telling men what to do." The latter trait manifested itself to fateful effect on several occasions. In the Cheat Mountain campaign of 1861, he accepted Loring's refusal to attack at Valley Mountain, and thereby lost an opportunity to win an important early victory for the South. At Second Manassas, he was prepared to tolerate Longstreet's several refusals to attack the exposed Federal left flank until the following day. On July 1, 1863 Longstreet again clashed with Lee when his recommendation of a movement around the left flank of Meade's army was rejected by his commanding general. Throughout the remainder of the battle at Gettysburg, Longstreet appeared to lack enthusiasm for the contest, which was tolerated by Lee. According to Douglas Freeman, Lee's weakness in this respect is explained by the fact that he had been brought up in genteel society where "kindly sentiments and consideration for the feelings of others were part of *noblesse oblige*… Detesting a quarrel as undignified and unworthy of a gentleman, he showed himself willing, in this new state of affairs, to go to almost any length, within the bounds of honor, to avoid a clash. In others this might have been a virtue; in him it was a positive weakness."

Although greatly respected as a strategist, Lee operated a devolved, if well considered, system of command. Always working through his corps commanders, he trusted the judgment of his subordinates as they were closer to the action and could react to changing circumstances. Such a system worked well while there existed an understanding between the commanding general and his fellow officers. Once that understanding began to break down, things could, and did, go badly wrong, as they did in the case of James Longstreet at

Gettysburg. In the final analysis, Robert E. Lee was very human and far more interesting than many traditional biographers and historians have portrayed. Although a product of his environment and childhood, circumstances conspired to ensure that he fought for his beliefs to the best of his ability for four long years, and he rightly deserves his place among the greatest military commanders in history.

WHEN WAR IS DONE

With Arlington taken as a military cemetery by the end of the Civil War, Robert E. Lee and his family returned to the house they had rented on East Franklin Street, Richmond, since 1864. Spending the first two months of the post-war period at that address, Lee was then offered free accommodation at "Derwent," an overseer's house on the plantation of family friend Thomas Cocke, near Cartersville, in Powhatan County, Virginia. The quiet of the country offered respite from an "endless file of visitors" who demanded the war-weary ex-Confederate commander's attention in the city.

Meanwhile, during June 1865, Judge John C. Underwood and a grand jury in the US district court at Norfolk, Virginia, indicted Jefferson Davis, Robert E. Lee, Alexander H. Stephens, and others for treason. However, ex-Confederate soldiers did not have to face trial, as General Grant had written to the authorities insisting that the parole given by him to the officers and men of the Army of Virginia at Appomattox should be respected. Regarding ex-President Davis, he was imprisoned for two years and then released on bail that was posted by prominent citizens of both Northern and Southern states. In December 1868, the court rejected a motion to nullify the indictment,

Immortalized mounted on Traveller by photographer Michael Miley in 1866, Lee was by this time President of Washington College in Lexington, Virginia. (The Museum of the Confederacy, Richmond, Virginia)

This chromolithograph by Strobridge & Company is based on post-Civil War photographs taken of Lee when he was president of Washington College in Lexington, Virginia. (Library of Congress – LC-USZC4-13351)

but the prosecution dropped the case in February 1869.

Growing fond of country life, Lee wrote his son Robert E. Lee, Jr. on July 29, 1865 that he wished to retire to a farm of his own with "some grass country" where he could live off "the natural product of the land." A few days later he received an offer to serve as president of Washington College, now Washington and Lee University, in Lexington, Virginia. Although he had already refused on denominational grounds the vice-chancellorship of the University of the South at Sewanee, Tennessee, and had rejected suggestions that he might connect himself with the University of Virginia, he accepted the position at Washington College and was president of that institution from October 2, 1865 until his death. His four-year experience as superintendent of West Point stood him in very good stead, and over a five-year period he transformed Washington College from a small, undistinguished school into one of the first US colleges to offer courses in journalism, business, and Spanish. He also imposed a simple concept of honor on its students, stating: "We have but one rule here, and it is that every student be a gentleman." Most significantly, Lee focused the college on attracting male students from the North as well as the South. As military instruction was also provided, Lee forwarded a request to the War Department in November 1865 for permission to retain "a few old United States pieces of artillery" at Lexington for use as gunnery practice. Clearly concerned about cannon once again under the direction of Robert E. Lee, Secretary of War Edwin Stanton promptly sent an officer to "convey the guns to Richmond."

On May 29, 1865, President Andrew Johnson issued a proclamation of amnesty and pardon to persons who had participated in the rebellion against the US. Although excluded from the 14 classes of ex-Confederates concerned, Lee sent an application to Grant on June 13, 1865 and wrote to President Johnson stating that he wished to apply for "the benefits, & full restoration of all rights & privileges." On October 2, 1865, the same day that he was inaugurated as president of Washington College, Lee signed his Amnesty Oath in front of Charles A. Davidson at the Office of Notary Public in Rockbridge County, Virginia, thereby complying fully with the provision of Johnson's proclamation. Unfortunately, the document he signed was "lost," and not recovered for 105 years when, in 1970, an archivist at the National Archives in Washington, DC, discovered it among State Department records. Thus, Lee died a stateless person. Finally, in 1975 he was posthumously reinstated as a US citizen by President Gerald Ford.

Lee experienced another heart attack in October 1869. Having never completely recovered from the heart problems suffered in 1863, he also struggled with muscular rheumatism of the back, right side, and arms. According to William Preston Johnston, a close friend and member of the Washington College faculty, "the flush upon the face was deepened, the rheumatism increased, and he was troubled with weariness and depression." Heeding the advice of doctors and friends to get away from the damp Virginia winter, he took a six-week sojourn in Georgia and Florida, during which time he visited the grave of his father at Dungeness, on Cumberland Island, off the coast of Georgia. Although benefiting from the Southern sun, the excessive traveling took its toll and he returned in a physical condition Johnston described as "not greatly improved." He also spent some summer weeks of 1870 at the Hot Springs in Bath County, Virginia, and returned home in better health and spirits to resume his collegiate duties that September. After chairing a long vestry meeting at the Grace Episcopal Church on September 28, 1870, he suffered a stroke. Bed-ridden, he died from the effects of pneumonia shortly after 9.00am on October 12, 1870 in Lexington, Virginia. He was buried beneath Lee Chapel at Washington and Lee University, where his body remains today. According to J. William Jones' *Personal Reminiscences, Anecdotes, and Letters of Gen. Robert E. Lee*, his last words on the day of his death were "Strike the tent" and "Tell Hill he must come up," but this may not have been the case as the stroke he suffered two weeks before resulted in aphasia, which deprived him of the power of speech for most of the time he lay dying.

Mary Randolph Custis Lee (1808–73) survived her husband by three years. She died at the age of 66 and is buried next to her husband in the Lee family crypt at Lee Chapel on the campus of Washington and Lee University. (New York Public Library)

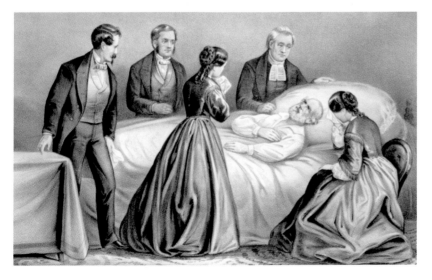

This Currier and Ives print depicting the death of Robert E. Lee on October 12, 1870 is inaccurate as it shows Custis Lee stood at the foot of the bed. Although telegraphed to come, none of Lee's three sons reached his bedside before he died. (Library of Congress – CPH 3B35219)

A LIFE IN WORDS

The death of Robert E. Lee was greeted with mixed comment by the press of the American nation. Typical of many Southern journals, the *Georgia Weekly Telegraph* eulogized on October 18, 1870: "The South, with streaming eyes and a sorely stricken heart, kneels today around a new-made grave. That grave awaits a tenant whose life, character and services in her cause have won for him as bright a chapter as glows on the glorious pages of her history, and whose hold upon the love and veneration of her sons and daughters was, and will ever be, her glory and his due." The day after the death of Lee, a correspondent for the radical Republican *New York Tribune* reported from Lexington, Virginia: "At the hotels, by the hearth-stone, in the schools, on the streets, everywhere, the only topic of conversation is the death of Gen. Lee. All classes of the community seem to be affected, even the colored people, who walk along in silence, with sorrowful countenance, and mourn the loss of 'Good ole Massa Robert.' Every house in the town seems to be draped with emblems of mourning, and no business has been transacted at any of the stores." In contrast, a short piece in the *Wooster Republican*, of Ohio, commented blandly: "Now that he is dead we shall only add that his body lies cold and powerless, while his record will live on and will forever be a blot and stain upon history's page."

The first literature produced about Robert E. Lee was influenced by the canon of the "Lost Cause," which sought to reconcile Southern white society to the defeat of the Confederacy. Possibly inspired by Lee himself, who referred to the "overwhelming resources and numbers" of the North when he published his farewell order to the ANV, those who contributed to this movement tended to portray the Confederate cause as noble, and most of its leaders as exemplars of old-fashioned chivalry who were defeated by the Federal armies not through superior military skill, but by larger forces.

The earliest extensive biography of Lee was written by James D. McCabe, Jr., and published in 1866. Entitled *Life and Campaigns of General Robert E. Lee*, it was grossly inaccurate in detail but useful for showing the esteem those closest to events held for their commander. Dedicated to Mary Custis Lee and published in 1872, the *Popular Life of General Robert Edward Lee* by Emily V. Mason (1815–1909), of Richmond, Virginia, was another early work to extol the bravery and virtues of General Lee. Five years earlier Mason had produced a compilation of poetry entitled *The Southern Poems of the War* containing at least six poems about Lee, which she hoped in her preface would help preserve "the hopes and triumphs and sorrows of a 'lost cause.'"

This collection of clothing and artifacts belonging to Robert E. Lee includes, from right to left: the coat worn, and sword carried, at Appomattox; boots and brass spurs; wartime saddle and saddle blanket bearing the motto "Honor to the Brave;" metal mess equipment and wooden carrying chest; camp table made by his African-American mess steward Bryan; English-made field glasses; Colt model 1851 Navy revolver; hat given to him by Rev. J. Clay Stiles; sword belt; and gilt brass Virginia belt plate. (The Museum of the Confederacy, Richmond, Virginia. Photography by Katherine Wetzel)

One of Lee's aides during the Civil War, Walter H. Taylor, wrote *Four Years with General Lee*, which was published in 1877. In support of the "Lost Cause" school of thought, Taylor was at pains to show the numerical weakness of the ANV at different stages of military operations, based on official documents held by the War Department at Washington, DC, many of which he originally produced during the war. Serving as chief of artillery in the Southern department during the winter of 1861–62, and as Lee's

secretary throughout the remainder of the Civil War, Armistead L. Long wrote the *Memoirs of Robert E. Lee* using a slate and stylus due to blindness in his latter years, which was published in two volumes in 1886. Regretful of the fact that Lee died before he could write his own memoirs, and much in the spirit of the "Lost Cause" literature, Long wished to make known his "personal knowledge of General Lee's life, actions, and character, and the part played by him in the great events of which he was the ruling spirit." In *Recollections and Letters of General Robert E. Lee*, published in 1904, his youngest son, Robert E. Lee, Jr., did much to further the cause with a subjective narrative heavily reliant on his father's letter archive.

A later manifestation of the "Lost Cause" mentality is found in the monumental four-volume *R. E. Lee: A Biography*, written by Pulitzer Prize winner Douglas Southall Freeman and published in 1934. While emphasizing the nobility of Lee's character, Freeman analyzes his mistakes, and agrees that not only superior numbers but fighting spirit contributed to the victory of the North. Included in more recent scholarship are two essential volumes that present the historical rather than mythical commander. Edited by Clifford Dowdey and Louis H. Manarin, *The Wartime Papers of R. E. Lee*, published in 1961, contain Lee's most important personal and military correspondence for the years 1861 through 1865. A second key volume is *Lee: The Soldier*, published in 1966 and edited by Gary W. Gallagher. This includes three memoranda on Lee's post-war conversations about his campaigns, plus numerous assessments of Lee made by modern and 19th-century historians. One of the most objective modern studies, *Robert E. Lee: A Biography*, was written in 1995 by Emory M. Thomas, retired Regents Professor of History at the University of Georgia. A very balanced work which is neither "classical nor revisionist," it relies solidly on thorough scholarship and a wealth of research into primary materials. The most recent interpretation is contained within *Robert E. Lee: Icon for a Nation* by British historian Brian Holden Reid, which looks beyond the legend to arrive at an objective assessment of the man and his military career.

The Lee Monument in Richmond, Virginia, was unveiled on May 29, 1890. For over 150,000 exuberant white Southerners looking on, only the name "Lee" was necessary on the base of the monument to identify the subject. (Virginia Historical Society)

SELECT BIBLIOGRAPHY

Blount, Jr., Roy, *Robert E. Lee*, Penguin Group: New York, 2006

Carrigan, Joseph G., *Cheat Mountain, or, Unwritten Chapter of the Late War. By a Member of the Bar, Fayettesville, Tenn.*, Albert B. Tavel: Nashville, Tennessee, 1885

Coddington, Edwin B., *The Gettysburg Campaign: A Study in Command*, Charles Scribner's Sons: New York, 1968

Cozzens, Peter, *General John Pope: A Life for the Nation*, University of Illinois Press: Chicago, 2000

Dowdey, Clifford, *Lee*, Little, Brown and Company: Boston, 1965

Dowdey, Clifford and Manarin, Louis H., *The Wartime Papers of R. E. Lee*, Bramhall House: New York, 1961

Freeman, Douglas Southall, *R. E. Lee: A Biography*, Scribner: New York 1934

Gallagher, Gary H. (ed.), *The First Day at Gettysburg*, The Kent State University Press: Kent, Ohio, 1992

———, *The Second Day at Gettysburg*, The Kent State University Press: Kent, Ohio, 1992

———, *The Third Day at Gettysburg and Beyond*, University of North Carolina Press: Chapel Hill, North Carolina, 1994

———, *Lee: The Soldier*, University of Nebraska Press: Lincoln, Nebraska, 1996

Jervey, Bird Pendleton, "Derwent in Powhatan County. And General Robert E. Lee's sojourn there in the summer of 1865" in *The Virginia Magazine of History and Biography*, Vol. 58, No. 1, January 1950

Jones, Archer, *Civil War Command and Strategy – The Process of Victory and Defeat*, The Free Press: New York, 1992

Jones, J. William, *Personal Reminiscences, Anecdotes, and Letters of Gen. Robert E. Lee*, D. Appleton and Company: New York, 1875

Lee, Jr., Robert E., *Recollections of General Robert E. Lee*, Archibald, Constable & Company: London, 1904

Long, Armistead L., *Memoirs of Robert E. Lee*, Low, Marston, Searle, and Rivington: London, 1886

Longstreet, James, *From Manassas to Appomattox*, Lippincott: Philadelphia, 1912

McCabe, Jr., James D., *Life and Campaigns of General Robert E. Lee*, National Publishing: St Louis, 1866

McPherson, James M., *Battle Cry of Freedom: The American Civil War*, Penguin Books: London, 1990

Mason, Emily V., *Popular Life of General Robert Edward Lee*, J. Murphy & co.: Baltimore, 1872

Nolan, Alan T., *Lee Considered: General Robert E. Lee and Civil War History*, University of North Carolina Press: Chapel Hill, North Carolina, 1991

Pfanz, Harry W., *Gettysburg – Culp's Hill and Cemetery Hill*, University of North Carolina Press: Chapel Hill, North Carolina, 1993

————, *Gettysburg – The Second Day,* University of North Carolina Press: Chapel Hill, North Carolina, 1987

Piston, William Garrett, *Lee's Tarnished Lieutenant: James Longstreet and His Place in Southern History,* University of Georgia Press: Athens, Georgia, 1987

Reid, Brian Holden, *Robert E. Lee: Icon for a Nation*, Weidenfeld and Nicolson: London, 2005

Schroeder, Patrick A. and Frantel, Scott, *Images of America: Appomattox County*, Arcadia Publishing: Charleston, South Carolina, 2009

Sifakis, Stewart, *Who Was Who in the Civil War,* Facts on File Publications: New York, 1988

Stewart, George R., *Pickett's Charge: A Microhistory of the Final Attack at Gettysburg, July 3, 1863,* Houghton Mifflin Company: Boston, 1987

Taylor, Walter H., *Four Years with General Lee*, D. Appleton and Company: New York, 1877

Thomas, Emory M., *Robert E. Lee: A Biography*, W. W. Norton and Company: New York, 1995

Tower, R. Lockwood with John S. Belmont, *Lee's Adjutant: The Wartime Letters of Colonel Walter Herron Taylor, 1862–1865*, University of South Carolina Press: Columbia, South Carolina, 1995

Woodworth, Steven E., *Davis & Lee at War*, University Press of Kansas: Lawrence, Kansas, 1995

Plus various newspapers, including the *New York Times*, *New York Tribune*, *Daily Dispatch* (Richmond, Virginia), *Richmond Examiner*, *Richmond Enquirer*, *The Telegraph* (Macon, Georgia), *Wooster Republican* (Ohio), and *The Sun* (Baltimore, Maryland).

INDEX